D1614416

THE STORY OF

BELFAST

AND

ITS SURROUNDINGS

First published in 1913 by

Headley Brothers, Bishopsgate, E.C.; and Ashford, Kent.

This edition published in 2009 by

Appletree Press Ltd
The Old Potato Station
14 Howard Street South
Belfast BT7 1AP
Tel: +44 (0) 28 90 24 30 74
Fax: +44 (0) 28 90 24 67 56
Web site: www.appletree.ie
Email: reception@appletree.ie

The text in this edition has been reproduced from the edition of 1913,
published in London by Headley Brothers.

Annotations and updates © Appletree Press, 2009
Editor for Appletree Press : Jim Black

The Story of Belfast and Its Surroundings

A catalogue record for this book is available from the British Library.

ISBN-13: 978-1-84758-147-1

9 8 7 6 5 4 3 2 1

AP3659

THE STORY OF

BELFAST

AND

ITS SURROUNDINGS

by
Mary Lowry
Author of "The Enchanted Portal", "The Clans of Ireland",
"Old Irish Laws and Customs", etc., etc., etc.

With over thirty illustrations

To
E. L.
Dear friend and comrade through
many pleasant years.

"The lot has fallen unto me in a fair land."

FOREWORD

The love of country is a virtue that we all need to possess, and this "Story of Belfast" tells us the author has it in abundance.

It is to this spirit of patriotism that we owe the following pages, and herein lies good fortune for us.

The story of Belfast and neighbourhood, comparatively short though its history may be, is nevertheless full of interest, and yet I fancy not widely known, and perhaps soon forgotten.

In these pages the author has endeavoured to rectify any such lack of knowledge on our part and has set up her story in such a manner as to compel a closer study of all that Belfast has to offer in the shape of history. Young, as well as old, are tempted to dip deep into this reservoir of historic fact and legend.

I feel confident that all who take advantage of the opportunities of study offered in these pages will find themselves well rewarded. The narrative is full of interest, recalling incidents and events, the reading of which will afford many pleasurable and instructive moments to those who have leisure for a perusal of its contents.

SHAFTESBURY.

Belfast Castle,
    Ireland.

ACKNOWLEDGEMENTS

I have to acknowledge with most grateful thanks the kindness I have received from the Right Honourable the Earl of Shaftesbury, and his courtesy in writing the preface for my book.

I must also thank the following, who have kindly given permission for the use of some of the illustrations in this book: The Committee and the Curator of the Belfast Art Gallery and Museum; Sir James Henderson; Mr. Ernest Hanford; Mr. A. R. Hogg; Mr. John Stevenson; Messrs. Macaw, Stevenson & Orr[1]; Mr. H. H. Mayne; Mr. J. J. Phillips, M.R.I.A.; Mr. R. M. Young, M.R.I.A.; Mr. A. C. Stannus; Mr. John Vinycomb, M.R.I.A.; and Messrs. Whitaker & Co.

I am also indebted to the Belfast Harbour Commissioners for the use of some rare and valuable books in their Library.

A list of books consulted in compiling this work will be found at the end.

MARY LOWRY.

INTRODUCTION

An ancient book tells us of "an old pleasant custom of our ancestors" who gave on the first page of a volume, "The place— the time—the author—and the cause of writing this book," so I shall follow the same old plan. The place—is high up on a hillside not very far from "The Eagle's Nest", where one can see over Belfast with its encircling hills, from Divis "The Mount of Sorrow", past Ben Madhigan's[1] lofty height and the long chain of hills above the ancient Castle of Carrickfergus, which still guards our Lough, and where Whitehead and Blackhead look across the Irish Sea. On this side the soft green hills of County Down form a foreground for the picture.

The time—in the last days of the dying year of 1912. The snow has fallen over the land, the giant face of the Cave Hill looks over a white world to-day, and earth has been washed clean and set to music.

The author—that matters least of all, but the author is one filled with a great love for her native land, and she wants all the young people to love it too, and to learn its story.

Now for the cause of writing this book.—It is strange how little the rising generation know about their own city. Belfast can boast of no very ancient history, but it has an interesting story to tell.

There have been many books written and many stories told

Introduction

about our city; but all for the "grown-ups". Now, if I can climb the Tree of Knowledge and shake the boughs again, perchance I may find some fruit still left that may be enjoyed by the younger people. If this small book of mine lives long enough to help anyone of the present time to understand and take an interest in the history of Belfast, I shall be more than satisfied.

CONTENTS

Contents

Contents

ILLUSTRATIONS

[The illustrations in this new edition of *The Story of Belfast and Its Surroundings* have been set in two 16-page sections: the first is found following page 64; the second following page 128.]

Illustrations

Illustrations

CHAPTER I

THE EARLY DAYS

This book is to tell the simple story of the places familiar to us all, for even the names of the streets have a meaning of their own. How many people know why Donegall Pass has such a curious name? For whom was St. Anne's Church named? It was *not* for Queen Anne. There were five Annes and five Arthurs in the Marquis of Donegall's family and that explains why these names were so frequently used in Belfast. How many know *why* there is a King John's Road in Holywood, and a King William's Road on the Holywood Hill? *Why* is there a "Joy" Street[1] in that particularly joyless neighbourhood, or a Fountain Street where no water is now seen?

Why should a road high and dry above the city be called The Falls? We shall find why these things are so in Belfast, and then see what is interesting in the places near us.

The first idea which suggested itself was to take the City Hall as a starting point, and in imagination take a walk along each road leading from it out to the suburbs. This is impossible, for in old times the place where the City Hall stands was surrounded with extensive fields and meadows for grazing, where we now have streets and houses.

We cannot go to the Lisburn Road or the Shore Road when there was no road there, so we must give up that plan and take the places as we can make the best out of them.

Belfast has no *very* ancient history as we know it in Ireland. Derry, Armagh, Newry, Carrickfergus and Bangor are richer in memories of the olden times, and these neighbouring places are filled with tales of thrilling interest.

Some one has truly said "Happy are the people who have no history"[2], and we know the best times are the years when nothing particular happens. So our fair city has been spared the bloodshed, the cruelties, and the destructions that were so painfully familiar to some more ancient cities.

It is mentioned in the "Four Masters"—a wonderful old book,—that there was a king's residence about ten miles from Belfast and a great fort called Rathmore about the year 680. A little while before that time, Bel-Feirste[3] was the scene of a battle which took place on the banks of the Lagan. St. Patrick was very near us when he was in County Down, but we are not told if he ever really came to Belfast.

The next mention of the town comes with the famous John De Courci, who arrived with a small army in the year 1177. He built a great many castles and churches, and lived in regal state in Downpatrick. He is said to have built the first castle in Belfast and a church where the old graveyard of Shankill is now. It was called the "White Church", and the "Chapel of the Ford" where St. George's Church now stands was a minor building.

De Courci was made the first Earl of Ulster, and he built twenty strong fortalices[4] round Strangford Lough, and great castles and churches at Ardglass and Greencastle, Dundrum, Antrim, and Grey Abbey all owe something to his masterful guiding hand.

King John next came in 1210. He arrived at Jordan's Castle in Ardglass on the 12th of July. He visited Dundrum, Downpatrick, and Carrickfergus and crossed the Lough to Holywood on the 29th of July, where the road he passed along is still known by his name. The O'Neills were for one thousand years great warriors in Ulster, and the story of that powerful family would fill volumes. One branch of the clan was intimately connected with Belfast, Clannaboy—Clan-Aod-Buide—children of yellow Hugh O'Neill.

The principal stronghold was the Grey Castle, at Castlereagh, which was in existence long before the name of Belfast was on any document, and was once called "The Eagle's Nest" from its situation and the powerful influence of Conn O'Neill. The coronation stone chair of the O'Neills is now in the Museum in College Square. It was found among the ruins of the Old Castle, and was brought to Belfast in the year 1755, but the chair of state had many adventures. It was built into the wall of the Butter Market. No doubt many a farmer's wife found it a resting place. Afterwards for some unknown reason it was taken to Sligo. Then it was brought back, and has found a home in the Belfast Museum. King Conn O'Neill has left his name at Connswater and Connsbridge. Many a story is told of him, and his end was very sad. He was imprisoned in Carrickfergus, but he managed to escape to Scotland. In order to save his life he was obliged to transfer his property to Sir James Hamilton and Sir Moses Hill[5], for he was the owner of 244 townlands. In the year 1606, he gave seven townlands to Sir Hugh Montgomery and seven to Sir Fulke Conway. His vast estates were taken from him, and he died in great poverty in a small house at Ballymenoch near Holywood. All the land as far as the eye could see had once belonged to him, and, at the end of life, he could claim only a grave in the old Church that once stood at Ballymachan.

Not a vestige of it now remains, but when "The Moat" was built some years ago several tombstones were taken out of the old graveyard which is now the orchard belonging to "The Moat". One of these stones bore traces of carving, and it is said to have been the top stone of Conn O'Neill's tomb. There was a leather pouch found in Westminster a hundred years ago. Inside the pouch was a taxation roll with "Hibernia" marked on it. The roll is dated 1307. Edward II. claimed the tenth of the ecclesiastical revenues of Ireland and an entry occurs "Ecclesia de Ballymichan 4 marks, £2 13s. 6d.", the valuation of that time. Several old writers mention the ancient church at Ballymachan, and it was there that poor Conn O'Neill found his last resting-place. His life was a long battle, and he never knew peace until he was laid in the quiet grave on the lovely hill-side at Belmont.

The changes that have taken place in Belfast seem now almost beyond belief. At an early period, when an open river ran down the centre of High Street, which was crossed by six bridges, the three principal buildings in the town were the Castle, where Castle Place is now, the market house at the corner of High Street and Corn Market, and the Church or Chapel of the Ford, where St. George's Church at present stands. Small thatched houses occupied the ground at each side of the river. Six hundred years ago, we are told that Belfast was a dismal swamp. Unrestrained tidal water mingled with two rivers, and floods of water from the mountains pouring down added to the swamp.

All higher ground was a primeval forest. The narrow point of land between the two rivers formed a peninsula on which the first buildings were erected from St. George's Church to Castle Street. The Blackstaff or Owynvarra flowed as a broad estuary into the Lagan, forming a complete defence for the south side of the Castle. It was crossed by an embankment made with piles, hence the Irish name "Owynvarra", "River of the Stake or Staff", changed afterwards to the English word Blackstaff, and the Forth River still runs down under High Street.

Let us take the three great buildings of three hundred and fifty years ago[6] and look at the contrast. The town in the year 1663 found that a Town Hall was required to keep up the "splendour and majesty of the town". So the upper part of the Market House was used and the yearly rent paid was the enormous sum of £5. The Lord Mayor of the time was for a great many years called the Sovereign, and his duties were decidedly varied, as we shall find later on. This Sovereign was regardless of the expenditure, for he ordered seats for the Corporation. One wonders how they did before the seats were made?

He made a "pair of stayres" adorned with His Majesty's Arms at the total cost of £20 16s. 9d. Considering that it was the *upper* part of the Market House that was used, the stairs appear to have been really required. The first Sovereign was appointed in the year 1612, and we have no record of where the Corporation met before the Market House was used. There was a Town Book kept from this time, but the early entries are very few, and but scanty information can be gathered from these shadowy records. The ancient book was in a dilapidated condition, worn out by constant use and want of care, and it was lost sight of altogether for many years. The Marquis of Donegall found it in a chest in his own house. He got it rebound, and it is now in Belfast.

In 1668, there was a tax levied by the Corporation of £4 to pay for a plush cushion, but we are not informed who used this cushion.

About the same time it was arranged that all the fines of Grand Juries and Petty Customs not exceeding ten shillings were to go towards keeping up the expenses of the Sovereign. This was repealed three years later, and a town purse was raised for his expenses. A curious perquisite[7] belonged to the Sovereign and there is no explanation of it to be found. Every butcher in the town who killed a cow was to give one tongue every week to the Sovereign, who must often have been thankful that cows generally have only one tongue; but even so, the diet would become monotonous. Four butchers once refused to pay this tribute—perhaps they were sorry for the Sovereign; but they had to pay twenty shillings and one tongue every week.

The Sovereign had to attend the Corporation Church every Sunday followed by the burgesses and freemen in state, and every person over thirteen years of age was obliged also to go to Church under a penalty of being fined in the sum of sixpence or up to five shillings, which was a serious amount in 1632. In this manner religious discipline was encouraged. Another curious law was enforced for a period of fifty-six years, that no Sovereign during the time he held office was to sell wine or spirits, or, if he did, a fine of £100 was enforced.

Evidently the Sovereign of Belfast was expected to set a good example, and his course of life was strictly marked out for him, including his Sunday behaviour.

"The Mace" had some curious adventures. It was made of silver, seven and a half inches long and it was hollow, with a round top, which was greatly disfigured and battered. On one side was engraved "The Burrogh of Belfast, 1639 C. R." and Charles I.'s motto and arms. After a long and mysterious disappearance, it was found in a pawnshop. History remains silent on this strange episode. Sometimes history is discreet, and we shall never know now who the sinner was who pawned the Town Mace. As Belfast grew in importance, so also did the Mace, for the next was seventeen inches long, made of silver with "W. R." engraved with the Royal arms and motto. The ball surmounting it has the rose, thistle, Irish harp and lily. The Baton is eight inches long, with a small crown on the top It was formerly carried by the town sergeant, but the Lord Mayor now carries it himself. The Town Seal was also lost, and another provided. A gold chain for the Mayor was presented by Lord Donegall in the year 1787. The badge has the arms of Chichester on one side, and the arms of Belfast on the other. This "Regalia" of Belfast has lately been replaced by articles of more imposing magnificence, and more suited to the dignity of the present City Hall.

The Sovereign had a pleasing variety in the performance of his duty. An advertisement in the year 1767 says "The Company at the Mill Gate will give a benefit to the Poor. Pit and Gallery 2s. 6d. each. The Sovereign will attend to take the tickets." But the most extraordinary order was issued and one that if suggested now would cause a tremendous commotion. He ordered that all swine wandering about the streets if not provided for by their owners in houses within five days would be destroyed. The keeping of pigs is still a troublesome matter in Belfast even in this twentieth century. Many a bye-law has been passed, but pigs continue to be kept. In the year 1768, the Sovereign applied a drastic remedy. Armed with a blunderbuss, he sallied forth on the 24th of October, 1768, and he shot two wandering, homeless pigs! Tired of the slaughter, he then offered a reward of thirteen pence for every porker slain! Imagine the picture! I wonder if he wore his robes of office and the golden chain and badge! Was he attended by the Town Councillors? Or did he stand lurking at the corner of Castle Place alone in all his glory to take deadly aim at the unfortunate animal?

If such a slaughter took place now, what a gala day it would be for the city. All the traffic would be stopped. Silence would reign supreme, and a long, long retinue of street arabs[8] and newspaper boys would watch and wait with bated breath until the fatal shot rang out and the misguided victim fell, his dead body a warning to all other erring swine. Imagination fails,—let us draw a curtain over the sad picture! With harrowed feelings we leave the touching scene.

On the whole, perhaps the City fathers have more important duties to perform now than collecting tickets at the Play House, or even the royal sport of boar hunting.

CHAPTER II
THE CHURCH

The first church of which we have any record was called the "Church of St. Patrick of the White Ford", and later on, it was known as Shankill, or the Old Church. It was a place of great importance, for we are told that it had six "Alterages" or small churches[1] attached to it, so Shankill was really the mother church of Belfast. There is not a vestige left now of the church, and an unsightly mound marks the spot where it once stood. The old graveyard is still very occasionally used by those families who possess a right of burial there, but the ground is more than full. The ancient font which lies in the graveyard is formed out of a solid block of stone about three feet square with a hole cut in it. This ancient font is now used by the children of the district for a very curious purpose, and it is looked upon with reverent awe, as it is believed that it has marvellous powers of healing. Any child who has a wart sticks a pin into it, and then drops the pin into the hole in the stone, and the wart is cured. How frequently this is done may be seen from the solid layers of pins lying in the stagnant water which half fills the cavity. The font, which dates from the year 1413, is now re-named the Wart Stone. In the year 1911, it was removed to St. Matthew's Church, and set up on a pedestal at the entrance door.

A curious old watch tower is still to be seen. It was built

for the watchmen who were there for the purpose of guarding any newly-made graves, and it recalls the horrors of the time of Burke and Hare, who were imitated in many large towns. When a funeral took place, the grave was opened and the dead body was taken out and sold to medical students at the College for dissection purposes.

The nearest church to Shankill was mentioned in 1306 as being one of the "Alterages". It was the "Chapel of the Ford", afterwards known as "The Corporation Church". It was the church to which the Sovereign and the members of the Town Council went in state on Sundays. We know it now as St. George's Church in High Street.

The old Chapel of the Ford was a small building close to the river. High tides flowed over the graveyard, and small boys used to sit on the wall and catch fish.

The Chapel of the Ford was largely used by travellers who entered the church to offer prayers for a safe journey before they dared to venture on the dangerous crossing of the river Lagan, for it was a hazardous undertaking in those days. We have no record of any returning travellers offering thanksgiving prayers when the danger was over. History is modest as well as silent on this point.

The old church weathered through many stormy scenes, and it shared the common fate of the country. It was broken down and repaired again and yet again, and was finally rebuilt as the Parish Church of Belfast. The graveyard was extensive and occupied a large square space, bounded by Church Lane, Ann Street, Forest Lane—now Victoria Street—and High Street. It was the principal burying place for the oldest families in Belfast, and many monuments were built along the inside of the boundary walls. It was here that the remains of the unfortunate Henry Joy McCracken were interred. Stirring times were those of the Cromwellian party, and the Protector left a trail of dire disaster wherever he went in Ireland. Cromwell did not come so far as Belfast. He never passed Drogheda, but he sent a strong force under the command of Colonel Venables to take possession of the town. He ordered Belfast to surrender, but Belfast refused, and he besieged the town for four days, when some agreement was made, and he entered the town. Old history states there was a short battle fought in some fields between the present Donegall Street and York Street. This was confirmed many years after when a cotton mill was built there, and marks of entrenchments were discovered, and also some cannon balls and ammunition found. This was the only time that Belfast was ever besieged. The Sovereign at that time was Mr. George Martin. He refused to find accommodation for Cromwell's army, so they destroyed his house and seized his property, and he was obliged to leave the country. Colonel Venables fortified the Corporation Church and re-named it "The Citadel". It was probably the most important building in the town, and the fact of its being a sacred edifice never cost the Cromwellians a single thought.

A curious scene took place one Sunday morning. Cromwell appointed the Rev. William Dix to preach, but another clergyman, the Rev. Henry Livingstone objected so strongly that he went up into the pulpit and forcibly ejected Mr. Dix, and we are not told who conducted the service on the following Sunday. Henry

Cromwell gave £100 afterwards towards the repairs of the church. After the Restoration, it was put into proper order, and remained until 1774 as the Corporation Church, when old age and infirmity rendered it unsafe, and all the privileges of the Parish Church were transferred to St. Anne's. The Marquis of Donegall built St. Anne's at his own expense, and also presented an organ. He spent £10,000 on the church and named it St. Anne's in memory of his beloved wife. St. George's was built upon the site of the old church in High Street, and the lofty pillars along the front were brought from Ballyscullion, one of the palaces built by the Earl of Bristol when he was Bishop of Derry. The long line of "Vicars of Belfast", as the incumbent of St. Anne's was termed, shows many very important names. The Rev. William Bristow was also Sovereign as well as Vicar. He held the position of Sovereign with such discretion and dignity during a most trying period of the town's history, that he was re-elected ten times. He preached the last sermon in St. George's as the old parish church, and also preached the first sermon in St. Anne's, the new parish church.

In the year 1801, we read of a curious circumstance, which would cause a great sensation if such were permitted now. Mr. Incledon, who was considered the greatest singer of his time, was engaged for nine nights. He offered to sing on behalf of the funds of the Poorhouse. The performance was held at three o'clock on Sunday when the church service was over, and a selection of sacred music from Handel's Oratorios was given in St. Anne's Church—"Admittance 3 British Shillings." We are told that the sum of £81 11s. 4d. was raised from this Sunday concert.

Another innovation occurred when a collection was taken for

the Poorhouse School. The five principal ladies in Belfast acted as collectors: The Marchioness of Donegall, Lady Mark Kerr, Lady Harriet Skeffington, Mrs. Dickson and Mrs. Drummond. They were attended by the Marquis of Donegall, Lord Mark Kerr, William Skeffington, General Drummond and the Sovereign. The amount of the collection proved most satisfactory, and we can well believe the attendance at church on that particular Sunday was also satisfactory.

St. Anne's still exists, but it is now known as St. Anne's Cathedral. The foundation stone of the new building was laid in 1889 by the late Countess of Shaftesbury. It is still in an unfinished state, but when it is completed it will be a very fine building.[2]

CHAPTER III

THE OLD CASTLE

We read of the Castle of Belfast as occupying a very important part in the old history of the town.

A Castle existed from the earliest times, but the arrival of John De Courci, in 1171, made a great change throughout the North of Ireland. He first conquered Downpatrick, where he lived in regal state, and he was the first Norman to take possession of Belfast and the country round. When he was created Earl of Ulster, it is supposed that he built the Castle, but this has not been verified. Another Earl of Ulster lived later on in the Castle. Belfast Castle was twice taken by the Earl of Kildare, and from 1503 to 1512 it was inhabited by Randolphus Lane. Then it belonged to the O'Neills, from whom it was taken, and afterwards restored. Queen Elizabeth claimed the right to grant the lands of Ulster to whom she liked. Being displeased with O'Neill, she gave Clannaboy and a great part of the country, including Belfast and the Castle, to Sir Thomas Smith and his son, who had all their duties set forth in a very lengthy document. One stipulation was that they were to be "firm and stable in their own strength, vigour and effect." However, the Smiths failed to carry out their part of the agreement, as they were weak and unstable, so their stay was a short one, and Belfast again reverted to O'Neill, the lawful owner.

O'Neill was elected as chief seated on his regal chair at

Castlereagh, and was knighted, but he was again unfortunate. Sir Arthur Chichester was appointed Governor of Carrickfergus in 1599. He was a wise and prudent man and from the time he appeared there was more peace for Ulster. James I. granted him the Castle of Belfast with a large portion of the lands surrounding, and he was made Baron of Belfast. This Lord Chichester was said to have been the finest man in the country, and from the time the Chichester—afterwards the Donegall—family became connected with Belfast, the town owed its prosperity to their wise and generous rule. Lord Chichester built a fine house in Carrickfergus, where he resided when Governor. Joymount, called for Lord Mountjoy, was designed by Inigo Jones and was a fair and stately mansion with gardens and a bowling green attached to it. He died in Carrickfergus and a tomb was erected to his memory in St. Nicholas' Church.

In 1611, the Castle of Belfast was built upon the site of the former Castle. It was surrounded with spacious gardens which extended from the river along to Cromac Woods and near Stranmillis. It is curious to read of hunting, hawking and other sports in the woods and meadows where now we have long streets of houses. The gardens, shady walks, orchards, bowling greens and cherry gardens are all gone, and nothing remains of the fish ponds. The stately palace, once the centre of hospitality and culture, is now only a memory. King William was received here in 1690. He admired the Castle and all its pleasure grounds and the beautiful gardens so much that he remained on a visit for five days. He received an address from the citizens and issued a proclamation "given at our Court at

Belfast." No other King ever visited Belfast again until the late King Edward VII. in 1903. The third Earl of Donegall was a soldier of great eminence and distinguished himself throughout the Spanish war[1]. He was unfortunately killed abroad, at the age of forty years. Two years later, in 1708, the Castle was burned to the ground, three of Lady Donegall's daughters were burnt to death, and two servants also perished. The Castle was never rebuilt, and the Marquis of Donegall lived for a time in Donegall House at the corner of Donegall Place.

Ormeau was also one of the residences, and it was there that the second Marquis died in 1844. He had also lived at Annadale. Nothing now remains of the old Castle except the names which mark where the strong, stately edifice once stood. It filled Castle Place, the principal entrance was where Castle Market is now, and the old courtyard had an entrance from Castle Lane. The bowling green extended from Church Lane to Corn Market, and what is now Ann Street was called the "Back of the Green". It was named not for Queen Anne, but for Anne, Lady Donegall. Lord Donegall's pleasure-boat was moored where Arthur Square is now. The open river of the Blackstaff flowed through Police Square into Hanover Dock, and May's Dock was called for Sir Edward May, who was the brother of Lady Donegall, and so we get May Street and Great Edward Street. Sir Edward May reclaimed the land to form May's Dock from the original bed of the river and the high water line was where Great Edward Street now continues into Cromac Street. The remains of the old toll house are still in existence between the corner of Great Edward Street and the new wall of the present market at the end of Chichester Street.

Belfast owes a great deal to the foresight and generosity of the Donegall family. The old Poorhouse received grants of land at a merely nominal rent, as did also the Belfast Academical Institution, the Brown Linen Hall and the White Linen Hall. Belfast never would have been the large and prosperous city it has become but for the practical interest successive generations of the Donegall family have shown in the place. The present Earl of Shaftesbury is the direct descendant of the third Marquis of Donegall, who had one son and one daughter. His son, Lord Belfast, died in the year 1853. His young life was full of promise for a brilliant career, he was exceptionally gifted and his early death was greatly deplored. His sister married Lord Shaftesbury and her son inherited the present Belfast Castle. The new residence is a large building on the side of Cave Hill, and the new Belfast Castle is like the old one, "a fair and stately mansion". The small private chapel belonging to the Castle is a gem of beauty, and the exquisite monument erected to the memory of Lord Belfast is not seen or known as it ought to be. Comparatively few Belfast people are aware that such a rare and beautiful piece of sculpture is in the little chapel on the slope of the Cave Hill.

CHAPTER IV

ORIGIN OF STREET NAMES

It is very interesting to trace the familiar names of the places we know back to the beginning and find the reason for some peculiar names. Ballymacarret means the town of McArt.

Wolfhill was a wild, lonely place where the last wolf was killed, but we may suppose that there must at one time have been more than one wolf in residence there, hence the name. The name of Crumlin Road is obvious, for it was simply the only road to Crumlin, and a hilly journey it was in the old times.

The Antrim Road is comparatively new. Carrick Hill was in ancient times called Carrickfergus Street, as it was then the direct road to the city of that name. The part called Carrickfergus Street is now known as North Queen Street. Carlisle Circus was named for the Earl of Carlisle, who was Viceroy of Ireland at the time it was planned.

Five Earls of Donegall in regular succession for one hundred and fifty years account for the name of "Arthur" being so frequently used, and five ladies of the Donegall family gave the name of "Anne" to a great many places.

One Lady Donegall was named Letitia, and Lettice Hill owes its name to her. It was then a famous country retreat, with orchards and gardens, near "My Lord's meadows", and the Lady

Letitia spent much leisure time there.

"Cow Lane", now Victoria Street, was where the cows were driven through when they were taken to graze on the Strand ground, and Goose Lane was named for a similar reason. Skipper Street was where the "skippers" or captains of the vessels lived, and it was then close to the docks.

Bridge Street was the principal bridge over the river in High Street, and it was here that the "May Pole" was a striking feature for many years. The last Maypole left remaining in Ireland is still to be seen in the High Street in Holywood. Church Street was so called from the old Corporation Church. It was formerly known as School-house Lane.

Bank Lane was once known as the "Bank of the River". Fountain Street was once called "Water Street", as it was there that the fountains were, that at one time supplied the town with water.

Hercules Street was named after Sir Hercules Langford, and Sugar House Entry from the sugar-refining industry which was carried on there. It was to No. 13 in this entry that the dead body of poor, ill-fated Henry Joy McCracken was carried by his friends, after he was hanged at the Market House in the year 1798.

Corn Market was once called the "Shambles". It was a favourite place for butchers' shops, and from the Plough Hotel, the last of the night mail coaches ran to Dublin. The memory of the name lingers still in the "Plough Buildings". Belfast Castle gave the name to many surrounding places, and Linen Hall Street was opened through the Castle Gardens when the Linen Hall was built. Old Forge and New Forge were named so, as they were used for smelting iron.

One of the most curious names remains with us in "The Donegall Pass". There was no road at one time between the Dublin and Ormeau Roads, but Lord Donegall opened six wide avenues through the woods, and they were known as the passes. Donegall Pass alone keeps the old name, and people were allowed to use the footpath through the trees "to pass" from one road to the other. Ormeau was built after the Castle in Castle Place was destroyed by fire. It was once a fine house beautifully situated on the bank of the Lagan, with spacious grounds and gardens, and some of the old trees now in the Ormeau Park may then have been the "young elms" that gave it the name of Ormeau.

The graveyard at Newtownbreda dates from the year 1180, and is still used.

Another very old place and name is "Friar's Bush" on the Stranmillis Road. It was once a monastery, but it owes the curious name to a holy friar, who was said to have been endowed with some miraculous powers, and it was beside the ancient tree in the centre of the graveyard that he performed his daily devotions, hence the name of "Friar's Bush". The inscription on his tombstone is "This stone Marks Ye Friar's Grave, A.D. 485", so he must have been one of the early disciples of St. Patrick, who had visited this place some time before.

From the great Cromac woods, on to Stranmillis, the country was stocked with deer, and was used for hunting and hawking. Cromack means bending or stooping, a winding river.

Malone Road was once called "Mylone", or "Myllon", "the plain of the lambs", and we find goats' whey and pure milk advertised to be sold at Donegall Pass, the "Throne" gardens, and at Millfield. The Falls Road gets its very curious name from the Irish words "Tuath-na-bhfal", district of the falls or hedges, and Castlereagh from the Grey Castle where King Conn O'Neill once lived. Waring Street was named from Thomas Waring, who had tanneries there in the year 1645. He made a curious will, leaving his wife "fifteen pounds a year, two rooms and the kitchen furniture, also the beds therein, one Sylver cupp, two best Sylver spoons, and one park of land near the North Gate." Waringstown is named for the same family. Thomas Waring had a son William, whose daughter, Jane Waring, was known as Dean Swift's "Varina". She refused to marry him, although it was said that he waited for her for four years.

Mustard Street was named from the mustard works there, and Mount-pottinger and Pottinger's Lane from the famous Pottinger family. Thomas Pottinger paid £20 a year rent for all of Ballymacarrett. It was once a forest, and from Queen's Bridge to the Rope Works at Connswater there were only two houses. May's Dock was the original bed of the Blackstaff River at the old Police Office, and it flowed into the Lagan at Queen's Bridge. Sir Edward May reclaimed all the ground along Great Edward Street, where the high-water line was.

A paved road from West Holywood is now called Strandtown. The Strand extended to Connswater and was crossed by a ford, and if continued in a straight line across the Lagan it comes out at Waring Street. Lord Avonmore reclaimed part of the causeway across the Strand. There was then no road through Ballymacarrett. Sixty years ago the Queen's Island was a public park with gardens and trees and a great Crystal Palace with a zoological collection.

The shallow water behind was used for bathing, and a row of bathing boxes was there, and there was also a bathing pond on the Lagan. Small ferry boats took people across the river for a charge of one halfpenny. Townsend Street was once the end of the town. North Street was the nursery for many well-known merchants. Callendar Street was where calico was calendered[1]. Hyde Park was named for a family called Hyde. In the year 1800, a row of small cottages thatched with straw, stood where the Commercial Buildings are now. Thatched houses were in Donegall Street and Corn Market. In 1810, there was a thatched house in High Street exactly where Messrs. Patterson's is now. It was two stories high, and was used as the Blind Asylum of the town.

The Vicarage House was at the corner of Talbot Street in the church yard, and the house of the Master of the Academy at the other side of the Church at Academy Street. In the year 1801, Donegall Street must have been a damp place, for a gravelled footpath was ordered to be made for the health of the soldiers, as "dry feet are of the utmost importance and wet ones a most fertile cause of disease for armies." It was paved from the Poorhouse to the Academy walls, and the upper part was surrounded by fields and trees. The old Rampart was still beyond the Academy. We read of a house to be let, 34, Castle Street, with a most elegant garden adjoining, abundant vegetables, well-stocked fruit and wall trees. There are some well-stocked fruit shops there now, but no "elegant gardens".

One Arthur Thompson, advertises his farm at Fountainville of over ten acres, and in the year 1802 it was worth £10 a year. A little higher up the Malone Road, Fruit Hill was let at £8 15s. for twelve acres. The Malone Turnpike was at the top of the hill where Mount Charles is now, and when the Lisburn Road was made it was moved lower down, and the old toll-house is still there. A good house was advertised in Smithfield Square with a field to graze two cows. It would be an expensive place to graze cows now!

A large house stood alone at the corner of York Street, which was built by the old Stevenson family, and it is now known as the Oueen's Hotel.

When rebuilding in High Street twenty-five years ago at Messrs. Greenfields, walls were found that were built of turf.

The last thatched house in Belfast was in Frederick Street, and it was said that Lord Edward Fitzgerald was hidden in the roof of it when a price was set upon his head, but no reward, however large, would have tempted the owner of the small thatched cottage to betray his visitor.

We must close this chapter with a very brief notice of the Long Bridge. Before it was built in 1682, people had to cross the Lagan by Shaw's Bridge or a ferry boat. The new bridge was a wonderful sight, for it was 2,562 feet long, and had twenty-one arches. Ten years after it was built seven arches fell in, weakened by Schomberg's heavy cannon passing over it, and a ship was driven up against it, thus completing the disaster.

Garmoyle, the well-known anchorage, is named from an old word meaning "heaps of fish".

Friday has been the market day in Belfast for over three hundred and twenty years. Where the Belfast Bank now stands at the end of Donegall Street was once known as "The Four Corners", and it was a favourite place for open-air meetings to be held.

CHAPTER V

WATER AND LIGHT

Two of the most important necessities of our daily life that make for health and comfort are water and light. We have become so accustomed to a plentiful supply of both, that we can scarcely imagine there was once a time when both were regarded as luxuries. For a great number of years, the open river running down the centre of High Street, the mill dams, and various springs and wells about the town sufficed for the supply of the people. In course of time the river became foul and unpleasant, and unfit for use of any kind, more like an open sewer, and every kind of filth was thrown into it. But we must not blame our forefathers too much, for, in those early days, there was no drainage or any means of carrying the waste of the town away, and the open river was there always ready to receive any rubbish. It was convenient, and it was close at hand.

In the year 1678, George McCartney was Sovereign, and we owe a great deal to his wisdom and foresight. He called a town meeting to consider what could be done to obtain a supply of good and wholesome water. It cost £250 to bring it in wooden pipes into the town, and three places were arranged where the inhabitants could get water. Of course, it had to be carried into the houses. Lady Donegall gave £40 towards this undertaking. This supply continued for many years, and then the pipes wore out, and, when a hard frost came on, the condition of the town was deplorable. Some springs were found to have an abundant supply. The water from Mundy's well in Sandy Row was brought into Fountain Street, and three fountains stood there for the use of poor people. Crowds of women and children were to be seen waiting for their turn at the fountains to fill their buckets and carry home the household supply. Water carts carried Cromac water to the better class houses, where it was sold at a penny for two pails full, and the tinkle of the water bells was heard through the streets. Hot and cold baths were not in great demand.

Holywood was a favourite watering place, and open-air bathing was common all along the shore where the County Down railway runs now. Later on, baths were opened at Lilliput, where Manson taught his pupils swimming.

There were also baths at Bower's Hill in North Street, and a curious arrangement was that each bather received a glass of punch after the bath, all for two shillings. The present Peter's Hill baths would doubtless become immensely popular if a glass of punch were given with every bath, only it would require to be free.

Next we read of a more ambitious effort, for water was conveyed by an open water course from Stranmillis and Malone, and the springs at Fountainville, to a great circular reservoir in a country lane, where trees and fields were round it. It was called the "Basin", and the Basin Lane was once a favourite walk out of the town. It is difficult to realise that Bankmore Street, where Marcus Ward's warehouse was built, is now the only memory of the water supply of early days, and the name of Bankmore lingers about the former reservoir.

The next improvement in the water supply was under the management of the Charitable Society. Then the next supply came from Solitude and Carr's Glen for the north side of the town, and later on from Woodburn and Carrickfergus. It was brought into the waterworks on Antrim Road, and, still later, from Stoneyford near Lisburn. As Belfast increased with such rapidity, it became necessary to have a much larger supply of water, and so our present water system was carefully thought out and carried to completion. Between Newcastle and Kilkeel, round a spur of Slieve Bingian, and across the river at Kilkeel into the Silent Valley, the river has been impounded and this valley forms one of the sources of Belfast's present water supply. The water is collected from an area 9,000 acres in extent, a reservoir is to be formed by an embankment across the valley, which is 520 yards long and 90 feet high, and the water covers 250 acres. The water is then conducted along the slopes of Slieve Bingian into the valley at Annalong. It flows through a tunnel beneath Slieve Donard and Thomas Mountain, and is carried into Belfast by syphons and conduits. A special reservoir is built 350 feet above the sea level.

When we compare our fine water supply now coming fresh and pure from the Mourne Mountains in an inexhaustible abundance, brought forty miles, we can scarcely imagine how people lived in the old days when they were glad to get it at one penny for two small buckets full. Thirty million gallons will come into Belfast every day when the scheme is completed.

Even more surprising is the change in the lighting of the town. The first attempt was made by a polite request that on very dark nights the householders would place a small candle in their windows to enable travellers to find their way. This illumination was not expected on nights of "Moonshine". It was a usual practice to arrange social entertainments for nights when the moon was visible. In the year 1761, a law was passed that every householder who paid £5 a year of rent should contribute to place lamps along the river in High Street. This was a wise suggestion, for it must have been a very unsafe place on dark nights. Later on, a law was passed that a "Lanthorn" should be hung on every alternate door or window on dark nights from the hour of six o'clock until ten. All respectable people were supposed to be in their own houses after ten o'clock. This law was to be enforced from twenty-ninth September until twenty-ninth of March. We are not told if the owners of the alternate houses were allowed to use their neighbour's light without any claim for payment. Eight years later, every house was to show a light or pay a fine of sixpence.

After a lapse of many years, when the White Linen Hall was used as a kind of People's Park, and Donegall Place was known as the "Flags", and was the fashionable promenade for the town, the military band performed for two hours in the central vacant place at the entrance gates. Sunday evening was the favourite time. It is natural to suppose that such a gay scene required more extensive illuminations than "Lanthorns" provided, so oil lamps were placed in the iron standards of the railings which enclosed the Linen Hall. An oil lamp burning every twenty yards all round the building made it a pleasant place, and shed a dim religious light over the crowds.

When gas lamps were substituted for the oil, it was considered a great step forward, and so it was, for the gas burned steadily except on the rare occasions of a street riot, when unruly boys thought it was a great joke to smash the lamps and leave the mob in total darkness.

Gas had one great advantage over the oil, for it burned as long as it was required, whereas the oil was an uncertain quantity, and lamps had a bad habit of going out and leaving a smoky wick to perfume the atmosphere with a very doubtful fragrance. It was an exciting evening when the streets were lighted with gas for the first time. The Town Council turned out to see the effect, and the members walked arm in arm along the streets admiring the illuminations and very proud indeed of such a brilliant town.

Now even gas is hiding its diminished radiance in presence of electric light. So we progress step by step, and who can foretell what the generations to come may use to light Belfast in the future? From the open river and the wooden pipes to our magnificent water supply of the present time, and from the small candle stuck in the window-pane to the great globes of light as bright as noon-day, is a wonderful change, and we pause to ask, what will come next?

CHAPTER VI

EARLY TRAVELLING

The first stage coach to Dublin was in the year 1752, and the journey occupied three days, but the roads were so bad that it could not go beyond Newry during the winter months.

Then in 1788, a coach was able to go to Dublin from Newry in twenty-six hours. The speed was so marvellous that it was called "The Newry Flying Coach", and the fare was 1s. 3d. a mile. However, as many people were afraid of such terrific speed, a post chaise could be hired at the curious price of 1s. 7½d. a mile, and the whole journey was performed in two days and a half. A mail coach ran from Belfast to Carrickfergus in the year 1811, and it held three or four inside passengers, and took two or three hours for the journey. It was a favourite amusement for the Belfast Academy boys to stand at St. Ann's Church gate and cheer the "Royal Oak" as it passed.

In 1803, it was considered a great advance in travelling, when a second coach was put on the road to Dublin, and thirty or forty people could travel at once. At this time ladies were carried to evening parties in sedan chairs.

Early in the nineteenth century, it must have been a curious sight when Mr. Bradshaw of Milecross used to drive a tandem through Smithfield. He had a home-made chariot—which, to say the least of it, was peculiar—it had a fire inside and a chimney for the smoke to get out through the top of the carriage. The speed was not very great, for it was drawn by two oxen.

The first railway in Ireland was projected and carried out by a clever engineer named Vignolles. In 1834 the line was opened from Dublin to Kingstown, and the first engine was the *Hibernian*. Vignolles met with great opposition, but he persevered, and the railway was a great success. He afterwards extended it to Dalkey, on the "atmospheric" system[1]. The railway from Belfast to Lisburn was the second line in Ireland, and it was opened in the year 1839. An unfortunate mistake occurred on the opening day, for the engine got off the line and sank in clay. However, it was soon made right, and for some time Lisburn was the limit. The trains were to go at five miles an hour, and it was even thought they might go at twelve miles with care on a well-laid railway line.

The Belfast and Holywood Railway was opened in 1846, and in 1848 another was made from Belfast to Ballymena. The railway system was gradually extended in all directions until at the present time Ireland is covered by a network of railway lines, bringing almost every part of the country into closer touch with the towns. The first tramway laid in Ireland was from Warrenpoint to Rostrevor. It was opened in the year 1877, and it is still in use. A great advance in travelling was made in 1883, when Mr. William Traill completed the first electric tramway in the world. He conquered many difficulties, and immense opposition, but at last he succeeded, and the electric line was opened from Portrush to Bushmills, and shortly afterwards extended to the Giant's Causeway. Scientific men came from all parts of the world to examine the first electric tramway. It gave satisfaction then, and continues to do so still.

The Mono-railway was also used in Ireland many years ago, and now the Gyroscopic railway[2] is the invention of another Irishman.

In the future, we may expect to see great discoveries in the conquest of the air. Irishmen, who have always been in the front rank of invention, have fresh laurels to gain in improvements in aeroplanes.

The first attempt in Belfast to travel through the air was made by a man named Livingstone, in the year 1825. He tried to make a balloon ascent for three successive days, and, on the evening of the third day, was successful. He went from the Infantry Barracks in Pinkerton's Row, to Fort William. There was intense excitement. His flight was eagerly followed by large crowds of people, and he was carried back to town amid great scenes of triumph.

I often think that we do not give sufficient honour to the early pioneers of our great inventions. They spent the best years of life and persevered through many difficulties and great opposition, often at large personal loss, but in the end succeeded in perfecting their discoveries. We should never forget what we owe to such men.

The pneumatic tyre is also the invention of a Belfast man. When the first bicycle was made in the year 1819, it was called a "dandy horse", and now-a-days one can easily imagine that the honour and glory of riding such a machine existed more in the imagination than in reality. However, when Dunlop's[3] pneumatic tyre was invented, bicycle riding became a pleasure. The first one was tried in 1867,—a solid tyre—but it was not a success. It was tried with variations again and again, but did not fulfil the desired idea. Mr. Dunlop took it up and worked until he produced the famous pneumatic tyre which is now in almost universal use for wheeled conveyances.

Mr. Dunlop began life as a veterinary surgeon in Belfast, but he gave up his profession after his great invention became successful. His tyres are now adapted to motor cars, carriages and all kinds of bicycles, and Dunlop's pneumatic tyres are known and used everywhere.

We owe the great improvement which has taken place in recent years in our roads to the skill of another Belfast man, Mr. MacAdam[4], who had a foundry in Townsend Street. He worked out an idea that revolutionised road-making. Up to his time the roads were made with unbroken boulder stones of different sizes, which made a very unsatisfactory road. He tried making a road by placing large hand-pitched stones in the bottom, and these were covered on the top by broken stones just small enough to pass through a two-inch ring. Later on, this was still further improved by laying smaller stones on the top and rolling with a heavy roller. Our latest roads are now made with a mixture of tar and pitch used with the stones, these roads are named "Tar Macadam". Macadamised roads are known and made all over the world and are called in every place by the name of our fellow-townsman.

CHAPTER VII

POST OFFICE

In the early part of the eighteenth century, there was no post office of any description in Belfast.

In 1702, the Collector of the Revenue had charge of the post bag, and postal messengers travelled on horseback from Dublin. They delivered the letter "bagge" to him and he distributed the letters to those to whom they were addressed, when they called for them. The riding postman was very uncertain in the delivery of letters, and sometimes the bag would be lost for a few days, and not unfrequently never turned up. When he was suspected of having anything of value in his bag, he would be stopped by footpads and robbed.

Then mail coaches were started and were found to be safer and quicker.

In 1739, the first Post Office was opened and the Collector of Revenue was superseded. The letters had to be called for at the Post Office, but ten years later, the uncalled-for[1] letters were sent out, and the old man who delivered them received one penny each for his payment.

In 1768, a six days post to Dublin was established, then later on it was three times a week, and postal service to Scotland twice a week. The mails were carried on an open boat from Donaghadee. The Post Office was frequently removed until it was settled in

Donegall Street, then Church Street, and finally to the Custom House, where it remained for many years.

It was frequently the case that every town had a "fool" in it. He was generally a quiet, harmless creature who lived on charity, and provided amusement for the people. Belfast had three or four of these poor creatures at one time.

One of them known as "Jimmy" was employed as a messenger about the markets, and he was sent one day with a basket full of Carrick herrings, but, on the way, he quite forgot where he was to take them to. Poor Jimmy was greatly puzzled to know what to do, but at last the brilliant idea entered his mind that if he posted them, they would be delivered at the right place, so he went to the Post Office and quietly and quickly slipped every herring into the box. He departed well pleased with himself, but history fails to tell us how well the Post-Master was pleased, and perhaps it is just as well that a veil is drawn over the rest of the story.

In 1795, the Post-Master put up a notice to this effect. "That Merchants were requested not to send little boys for letters, but to send proper persons, as little boys behaved very badly and gave great annoyance to the Post-Master who could not be accountable for their conduct."

I wonder if the little boys of the present time behave any better, for it seems to be a very old fashion for boys to amuse themselves. It is a way they have.

There is scarcely any department of daily life in which there is a more marked improvement than in our postal system. The frequency, regularity and safety of the Post Office is a marvellous advance.

The first telegraph was suggested in the year 1804, the projector saying that he would communicate between the light-houses of Donaghadee and Portpatrick, and work as well at night as by daylight, but would keep his method a secret to himself, and he was allowed to do so. The telegraph system has made enormous strides during the past fifty years, and now the whole world is encircled in with the electric wires. Truly there is nothing new under the sun, and an ancient prediction made by Confucius in China when the world was young, has been fulfilled. He said that some day knowledge would run round the earth on the top of sticks. In those far-off days, he must have conjured up in his mental vision a dream of telegraph poles. Now we have the even more wonderful wireless telegraphy, which is the invention of Marconi, whose mother was an Irishwoman, and it is said that he once resided in Ballycastle.

The telephone is also one of the greatest inventions of the present time, and we hold our breath and wonder what will come next.

CHAPTER VIII

EDUCATION

Belfast was a very small place indeed, and it is much to the credit of the inhabitants that so long ago as the year 1647, we find references to the payment of a schoolmaster. A year later, a sum of £10 was to be raised every year by a tax on the people, to be paid for the maintenance of a schoolmaster for the education of the youth of the town. He was also to have a chamber to live in, and a suitable house for the school. It is a pity that history has left no record of the first master's name.

Later on, two teachers were paid by the Government, and they received £20 each as yearly stipend.

The Marquis of Donegall built the first school-house, which was either inside the churchyard, or very close to it, at the corner of Ann Street. Church Lane was then called Schoolhouse Lane. He afterwards established a Classical School for poor scholars, and, about the same time, he presented a Mathematical Lectureship to Trinity College in Dublin, and the endowment of £30 a year is still paid to keep it up. The master and scholars of the Classical School presented an address in Latin to the Marquis upon one occasion, to which he replied in Latin. Several schools sprang up and flourished as the town increased.

David Manson was the most famous schoolmaster of those early days, and he was the author of a very good dictionary, which is still known as "Manson's Spelling Book". He opened an evening school in Clugston's Entry in 1755, and his advertisement shows an amount of originality which is very pleasing.

He wishes his "customers" to know that he "teacheth by way of amusement, English Grammar, Reading and Spelling at moderate expense."

Five years later he removed to a front house in High Street, when he again announced in the quaint language of the time that he "will teach to spell, read and understand the English Tongue, *without* the discipline of the rod, by intermixing pleasureable and healthful exercise with instruction." One item in this advertisement must have appealed strongly to the youth of the town, for we find that in a short time he had to remove to still more commodious premises. He built a house in Donegall Street, "where there is a healthful air and delightful prospect of land and water." David Manson was a man whose ideas were much in advance of his time, for he combined games with his teaching, and had a bowling green at Lilliput for the amusement of his "good boys", and used the grounds of the Linen Hall for other sports. He invented a curious machine called "a flying coach" and a turn in it was the highest reward for work well done. Was this the forerunner of aviation?

Manson's flying coach was the embryo of the present airship, just as the "dandy horse" of long ago was of the bicycle.

The Belfast Academy was opened in the year 1786, and it has had a long and honourable history. Many of our finest public men have been educated within the old walls of the school in Academy Street, and for many years it was considered to be the first school in Ulster. The original building became too small for the increasing number of scholars, and, in the year 1876, the school was removed to the present very fine building at Cliftonville, where the Belfast Academy still holds a high place among the educational establishments of the city.

The story of the Academy cannot be complete without a brief notice of an event which is detailed at great length in one of the old books of the school records. Some real or fancied grievance roused the wrath of the boys and they took the law into their own hands. On the morning of the 12th of April, 1792, eight boarders and two day-scholars shut themselves into the mathematical schoolroom, and declared war against the masters until their requests should be granted. In anticipation of a prolonged siege, they had liberally helped themselves to a large quantity of provisions from the kitchen. They had also procured five pistols, and an unlimited supply of powder and shot, and were fully prepared for serious operations. They sent a written despatch headed "Liberty Hall" stating fully their demands and refusing to surrender until their requests were granted. Smiths were brought to break open the door. Slaters were sent up to the roof to pour water down the chimney, but all had to retire before the reckless firing of the boys.

At last the Sovereign was sent for to recite the terrors of the law, but the uproar of the battle continued all day, until late at night the unruly boys capitulated. We have no distinct record of the after events, and one would like to know if the boys were "disciplined with the rod" or were forgiven.

A few years later the famous "barring out" took place in

the college at Armagh, but that was a more serious affair and lasted for some time. The story of that exciting event belongs to another history.

Another popular school was in a place called Crown Entry, and it was kept by Mr. James Sheridan Knowles about the year 1812. He was a great elocutionist, and no record of Belfast schools could be complete without his well-known name.

About the year 1806, the first suggestion of higher education for the youth—both boys and girls—of the town was made. A year later, at a meeting held in the Exchange to consider the question, £3,000 was subscribed in a very short time. The idea of a great academical institution was enthusiastically taken up by all the influential people in the country adjoining.

Some delay occurred, but at last eight acres of waste ground were procured on the most liberal terms from Lord Donegall and the Institution was built upon a very desolate and dreary place. Nothing but wet grass fields like a dismal swamp lay round the new building, and a watchman was kept to drive stray cattle off the grass. Mr. James Thompson was the first Master of the Mathematical School, and Mr. James Knowles, Master of the English School.

For many years, it was known as the Belfast College, and many distinguished men were educated there. Mr. Thompson's two sons were amongst the most illustrious names. He built the first two houses in College Square East, which stood alone, fronting an open plain, with the blue encircling hills in the distance, and quite unsheltered from the blast. It was here that Lord Kelvin and Sir James Thompson spent their early days, and it is interesting now to read of them gathering flowers in the meadows round the Institution, of the buttercups and daisies and the beautiful summer sunshine where the children played in the breezy open fields.

It would not be treating the girls of Belfast fairly to allow the thought that all the education was considered to be for the boys' advantage. So it is pleasant reading to meet with an advertisement as follows, in the year 1755. "Mrs. Smith has given up her boarding school in Belfast, and is succeeded by Mrs. Lanagan, who teaches all manner of cookery, and the French language if desired." This indicates a pleasing variety in the course of study at Mrs. Lanagan's. Next we find Margaret Cullen in Dazell's Row opened another cookery school, and she "proposes to attend ladies at their own houses who prefer home instruction to the public school."

Two cookery schools! Was it all French cookery? Surely the ladies of the town were thoroughly well trained in the useful as well as the ornamental side of life.

CHAPTER IX

HOSPITALS

One thousand years ago there was a curious old Brehon law directing the people of Ireland how the hospitals should be built. There were a great many hospitals all over the country; poverty and sickness always appealed to the tender sympathy of Irish people.

Every hospital was to have four doors open for ventilation, and a stream of pure water was to run across the middle of each floor. It was to be kept very clean and no untidy habits were allowed. It was to be kept extremely quiet, and no noise or conversation was to be permitted. Hospitals were open to all classes, and poor people were admitted free, but those who were able to pay were expected to do so.

It seems to have been a very old fashion for wise men to believe in the virtues of fresh air and pure water. What was good for the people one thousand years ago still holds good for us in these later days. Truly there is nothing new under the sun.

There was a great hospital at "Emain", Armagh, in very early times. It was called by a beautiful name, "Broinberg", the "House of Sorrow".

In the year 637 A.D., we read of an operation being performed, which doctors now called "trephining". There was a great man, Cennfaelad, "Kenfaila", who had his skull severely injured in

61

battle. He was a year in Tomregan Medical School, and part of his brain was removed. The strange part of it was that he became so learned that he was afterwards named "Kenfaila, the Learned"; he never forgot anything, for the doctors had removed the bump of forgetfulness when his brain was opened. That operation is not often done now.

There were a great many places for leprosy throughout Ireland, for it was once a very common disease, but one we very rarely find here now. Perhaps at some future time, people may say the same about consumption[1], and it, too, may become a disease of the past.

We read that in the year 1651, Cromwell allowed a doctor and an apothecary to be engaged in Belfast if they were required, but on no account was the doctor to receive more than £100 a year, or the apothecary more than £60.

"The Old Poorhouse" was the first to give organised relief to the poor, but this was not sufficient for the purpose. It was at first intended to have thirty-six on the Poorhouse side, and twenty-four in the Infirmary, but this was afterwards changed and twenty poor children taken in.

In the year 1792, a Charitable Dispensary was opened to attend the poor in their own homes. A physician and surgeon attended three times a week.

The ladies of Belfast formed a society of their own in the year 1793 for the help of poor women, and they were so much in earnest that in less than one month, from the date of their first meeting, they had taken a house and begun work. The ladies of Belfast have generally been able to accomplish anything of a similar nature when they desire it.

In 1830, the Maternity Hospital in Clifton Street was built, and the work is now carried on in the larger Hospital in Townsend Street.

In 1793, a Fever Hospital was opened with six beds, and from this small beginning the Frederick Street Hospital was opened in 1817, which has now developed into the splendid Royal Victoria Hospital of the present day, and there are also many smaller special Hospitals throughout the city.

The Frederick Street Hospital was built for seventy beds, and thirty were set apart for fever. Epidemics of fever frequently swept over the town and all the beds were filled with typhus fever patients, often far more than double the number the place was intended to hold.

It was a serious consideration to accept patients for operations in the same building where typhus was treated, so, in 1846, a Fever Hospital was opened at the Workhouse, and all fever cases were sent there. Now we have a most up-to-date Infectious Diseases Hospital built outside the city, in the pure country air of Purdysburn. At present it has 168 beds.

The Workhouse Infirmary has 1,500 beds, for fever 100 and for children 200.

The first Medical School was in the Royal Academical Institution in the year 1835, and continued there until the Queen's College was built in 1849. The Medical School of Queen's has produced some very famous men, and has a record of which Belfast is most justly proud.

The Royal Victoria Hospital in Grosvenor Road was opened by King Edward in the year 1903. It occupies a site of six acres, and is fitted with every modern improvement for the relief and comfort of suffering humanity.

It is a marvellous change now from the days of Louis XVI., when he set to work to improve the French hospitals, and they must have required it. In Paris three patients were kept in one bed, but that was a decided step in advance from one hundred years before then, when six patients were accommodated in one bed. Now Paris has the most advanced hospitals and a splendid medical school. All over the world there is no other profession so ready to give their skilful knowledge, and patient care and attention, often for very poor reward. The old Irish system of payment was four shillings a day for surgeons and one shilling a day for nurses. With the advance of knowledge this has also been changed.

BELFAST, FROM CASTLEREAGH.

THE EARL OF BELFAST.
DIED 1853.

ANNA, SECOND MARCHIONESS OF DONEGALL.
DIED 1849.

The Friar's Grave, Friar's Bush,
Stranmillis Road, Belfast. Date, 483 A.D.

Baptismal Font. Used in the old church of Shankill, the first church
in Belfast, built about 500 A.D. Also called 'The Wart Stone'.

HIGH STREET, BELFAST, IN 1839.

FROM 'IRELAND ILLUSTRATED'. BARTLETT, PETRIE AND BAYNES.

OLD CASTLE, ORMEAU, BELFAST.

OLD TURNPIKE TOLL HOUSE AT JUNCTION OF LISBURN AND MALONE ROADS, BELFAST.

Thatched house, Frederick Street, Belfast. It was in the roof of this house that Lord Edward Fitzgerald was kept safely hidden in 1798, when a price was set upon his head.

OLD TOLL HOUSE at corner of GREAT EDWARD STREET and CHICHESTER STREET, BELFAST.
THERE WAS A DOCK HERE, AND EVERY VESSEL THAT CAME UP THE RIVER PAID TOLL AT THIS HOUSE.

ALBERT MEMORIAL, HIGH STREET, BELFAST.

THE GREEN LINEN MARKET AND COMMERCIAL BUILDINGS, BELFAST, 1839.
FROM 'IRELAND ILLUSTRATED', BY W.H. BARTLETT, C. PETRIE AND T.M. BAYNES.

OLD HIGH STREET, BELFAST, 1730.
SHOWING MARKET HOUSE.

VOLUNTEER REVIEW IN HIGH STREET, BELFAST.
ABOUT 1780.

The Rout of the MacGilmores, Cave Hill, Belfast.
Fifteenth Century.

JOY'S PAPER MILL, BELFAST.
1800.

MR. JOHN McNICHOLL WITH HIS WEB OF LINEN.
OLD BROWN LINEN HALL, BELFAST.

CITY HALL, BELFAST.
FROM A PHOTOGRAPH BY MR. A. R. HOGG.

CHAPTER X

THE BELFAST CHARITABLE SOCIETY

This is the oldest charitable institution in the city, and it has had a varied and most interesting career. It is perhaps better known at the present time as the "Old Poorhouse", and now after a record of over one hundred and fifty years' work, it is still one of the most useful and well-managed institutions we have.

The idea originated about the year 1752. There were at that time a great many very deserving poor people in the town, and it was considered that something ought to be done for their relief. A number of beggars crowded into the streets; they were a continual source of annoyance, and it was suggested that they should do some useful work in the Poorhouse. In the prospectus issued, it was at first proposed to unite three objects at once, but this was found to be unworkable. This was to rebuild the church, to build a Poorhouse, and to combine a hospital for the aged and infirm poor, and the money was to be raised by a public lottery, which was a common method of raising money at that time. Great difficulties arose, and caused delay, but at last, from varied sources, a sum of £7,500 was available, the church part of the scheme was dropped out, and the Poorhouse was planned.

Lord Donegall, to whose generosity Belfast owes so much, gave a grant in perpetuity of a most suitable piece of ground in an open, airy, healthy place. The gift of eight acres of land was indeed a handsome present, and, after some delay, the foundation stone was laid, in the year 1771. The eight acres have now increased to nineteen by additions granted by later members of the Donegall family, for which the society pays a nominal rent of £12 a year.

The beggars at that time were allowed to wear a badge and they were called "bang beggars". They were licensed to beg for a limited time. They became so numerous that some means had to be taken to reduce their numbers, and a sum of 5s. 6d. was paid for every beggar caught and brought to the Poorhouse. This was found to be a sad mistake, for the "bang beggars" brought up their less fortunate unlicensed neighbours and claimed the reward, so other means had to be adopted.

The poor had to work, and one beneficent plan was tried, but after a time was discontinued. This was, that husband and wife were allowed to live together. Then poor children were admitted, and it was in the Poorhouse that Mr. Joy taught the children the cotton manufacturing industry.

The methods adopted for raising money were many and various, and one curious item is a fee of £1 1s. a year for the use of a shower bath, quite an exciting recreation in the days of long ago.

There was a ball once a month and concerts once a fortnight. The sum of £250 a year was raised for the Poorhouse by these entertainments.

In the year 1772, a special collection was taken by ten ladies in St. Anne's Church in aid of the institution for female infant orphans. Rev. W. B. Kirwan, D.D., preached, and the ten ladies collected £752. In later years, about 1812, the House of Industry refused to accept the money raised by an amateur theatrical performance on the ground that it was sinful to accept money acquired by such means. Times have indeed changed since then, and no hospitals in town now refuse to accept money from such a source.

The "Old Poorhouse" has been a distinct feature in the history of Belfast for a very long time, and it is an institution that has the good wishes of the entire community.

CHAPTER XI

SOME CURIOUS LAWS AND TAXES

A great change has taken place in the value of money which it is well for us to understand when we read of what may appear to us now to be a very small sum. In the year 1575, £94 9s. 6d. was equal to £3,000 of our money at the present time[1]. If some kindly friend gave a small boy then a tip of one shilling, it would be quite a fortune, while half-a-crown would be beyond imagination. In the year 1636, chimneys must have been a curious sight, for they were made of straw bound together with hoops. Next, wooden ones were made, but so many fires took place that an order was issued that every chimney was to be built of brick. In 1660, Belfast was a small place with only five streets and five lanes and one hundred and fifty houses, but the town spread out and increased rapidly every year afterwards.

The "hearth money" tax was very old in England, and it was imposed in Ireland by Charles II., in 1666.

The ancient roll of names of those who paid this tax is still in existence, and it is kept in the Record Office in Dublin. It is, of course, in a damaged condition, but the list of names is very interesting.

All the money that was raised by the hearth tax was £28 10s. The very poor were allowed freedom from payment. Lord Donegall had forty hearths, the largest number in any house in Ireland. The Earl of Meath built a house in Dublin which was considered to be a very grand one, and it had twenty-seven chimneys. After Lord Donegall's name there were only two houses in Belfast which had four, nine had three, eighteen had two, and all the others only one each.

In the year 1798, during the rebellion, the town was guarded, all business was suspended and military law was ordered. Six men were brought into Belfast and hanged at the Market House, one on a lamp post, and the heads were placed on poles and left to blacken in the sun. The year 1798 was followed by two of the worst years ever known in Ireland, for there were heavy snowstorms, the most severe being in April, 1799, followed by constant rain and great floods, and the crops were destroyed. There was a proclamation issued that none but brown bread was to be eaten, and rich people were to have no second course at dinner, and the soldiers were forbidden to wear any hair powder. All the money possible was to be given to the poor. A generous collection was made for a soup kitchen, nine tickets were sold for one shilling and a penny, which were to be distributed to the poor. Each ticket allowed one quart of soup and one pennyworth of bread. Card tables were asked to double the sums left for cards. Dances and other amusements were asked for one shilling for each guest. Theatre tickets were sixpence extra, and all the money thus raised was to be used for the benefit of the poor. The soup kitchen was closed in December. The next year was worse, for 1800 was so dry. The ground was parched, and no rain fell. These two years were long remembered as the wet year and the dry one. In 1801, Ireland was in a most miserable condition, for there was no old seed stock for supply.

We may go back a few years, and notice a curious tax which was levied in 1773. Absentee landlords, who were away from their landed property for six months in the year, were ordered to pay a tax of two shillings in every one pound of rent. In 1792, no carter was to travel on Sunday under a fine of twenty shillings, or two hours in the stocks. I expect carters did not often travel on a second Sunday. The year 1800 seemed to be notable for quite a number of new regulations. All wandering swine were to be taken for the use and benefit of the Old Poorhouse. A water tax of forty shillings a year was to be paid on one house. If there was no water supplied for three days, only one fourth was to be paid.

There were no burials to be allowed to take place in St. George's graveyard, under a fine of from five to twenty pounds.

The rates appear to have been very fairly arranged, for houses paying from five to twenty pounds rent, were to pay sixpence in the pound, from twenty to eighty rental, one shilling in the pound, and all over eighty to pay one shilling and fourpence. Houses unoccupied for six months were not to pay any taxes. Churches, Public Charities and Foundations for Education were all declared free of taxation. An act was passed in 1800 for paving, lighting, and for keeping a night watch, and the streets were to be widened, cleaned and improved, but not more than £1000 was to be spent in one year.

Gunpowder was to be kept locked in a separate place, and if not so kept a fine of £10 was to be enforced. It was also to be sold only in daylight, under a fine of £10. No fires were allowed on board ships in dock on *any pretence whatever*, or a fine of £5 had to be paid.

The street lamps were well protected by law, and very severe punishment was given for injury done to them. The penalty for breaking, extinguishing or injuring a street lamp, was one to six months' imprisonment *without* bail. Anyone found stealing or carrying away any part of a lamp, might be found guilty of felony, and transported for seven years, or publicly whipped, at the judge's discretion. For training horses on the streets, a fine was imposed of from five to twenty shillings, and there was the same fine also for throwing dust, ashes, or rubbish on the street. Two masons struck work, and were sent to gaol for three months, which seems to have been a very severe way to deal with a strike. In the same year—1800—six shoemakers combined to have their wages raised, and they were at once sent to Carrickfergus Gaol, the judge remarking, "How could trade go on or trade improve if such actions were permitted?"

Beggars were obliged to wear badges, as so many foreign beggars came to Belfast in the year 1806.

Two men were hanged in front of Bank Buildings in 1816, for burglary. Our prison was at that time the House of Correction, which was built in 1803, in Howard Street. It stood then among green fields, and on the stone over the front door was carved this warning—"Within amend, Without beware." Serious offenders were sent to Carrickfergus Gaol, until our County Prison was built on the Crumlin Road. In the early days, one stipendiary Magistrate sat every second day in the Police Court, and there were two constables. The Police Office was in Rosemary Street. The old fashion of carving on the front of a prison was revived recently when the new Bridewell was built in Dublin. It bears across the front this polite apology, "Fiat justitia, ruat coelum", which translated means "Let justice be done, though the heavens should fall."

CHAPTER XII

QUAINT DOCUMENTS

It certainly was a curious custom when public auctions were advertised as follows: "Auction, to be sold by 'Inch of Candle[1],' 7 bales of tobacco and 7 ankers[2] of rum."

The Old Sugar House Company offered £52 10s. reward to find out who raised the report that a man fell into a pan of sugar and was boiled to death, and that the sugar was afterwards sold. It is difficult to trace such reports home, and the fifty guineas were never claimed.

There was a Bachelors' Annuity Company in the Market House, but we are not given much information about it.

A most polite advertisement appeared in the papers. "Woulf the Dentist leaves Belfast, but his partner, Mr. Sigmond, will remain for a year longer if he gets encouragement, though, at the same time, he must confess that no ladies he ever knew stood in less need of his assistance or the aid of any art." I wonder if he removed to Blarney.

Some of the old accounts belonging to the Donegall family give us a curious insight into the cost of living in the year 1666; for instance, sixteen yards of "mattin" were used in settling "My Lord and Lady's seat in church." It seems a considerable quantity, but, as it only cost twopence a yard, it really was not expensive.

Again, by my Lady's order, Mr. Charles was supplied with a

new grammar at 2*s*. 8*d*. He was eighteen years of age at this time. The summer suit for Mr. Charles was certainly not an extravagant item, for it only cost 7*s*. 1½*d*. Boots, shoes and goloshes[3] for my Lord cost £1 1*s*.

In the year 1800, there was a house advertised to be let in Mill Street, with a splendid walled-in garden.

The "Plains"—now covered with houses—Botanic Avenue, University Street and College Green, with the streets adjoining, consisting of twenty-two acres, was let at a yearly rent of £40 free of tithe, as in the past ages this ground was all church lands and was attached to the houses and Monastery at Friar's Bush.

We read also of a curious sepulchre at a place named "Crucmaur", but I cannot find out exactly where it is, and I am sure there are many people who would also be pleased to know. This place exactly fits the size of any person who lies down in it, and a weary pilgrim who kneels three times upon it, is never weary again. There are many weary pilgrims who would like to try it.

There are some interesting and amusing old wills recorded, one made in the year 1655, in which Thomas Dobbin leaves to Alice Dobbin's children one half-crown to be equally divided among them, share and share alike, and the same sum and same manner of division for the children of his two sisters, when they come to demand it.

I wonder how many children there were, and if they had far to travel to receive their share.

But we are surprised at the generous spirit shown by John Taylor, for he left his wife two silver spoons "that were formerly her own." John Taylor could not very conveniently take them with him. I do not think silver spoons were required in the land he was going to, and certainly the lady they belonged to had the best right to them. Another man left his old cloak to a friend, but he distinctly says "the one with the patch on the corner." I trust this bequest was valued as highly as it ought to have been—patch and all.

How the times have changed since those early days! We cannot imagine the astonishment of our great-grandparents, if those venerable people could revisit the haunts of their youth, and see the motors, the telephones and so many surprising things, and perhaps among the most bewildering would be the twentieth-century ladies. The calm serenity of life long ago must have had a pleasant side, for they had time to live then, and time to enjoy living in a way we cannot do now. We attempt to fill life too full, we put too much into the time we have, and, when the end comes, we leave the best undone.

CHAPTER XIII

THE HARBOUR

The harbour of Belfast had indeed a very small beginning, and the original dock or "Creek", as it was called, was the mouth of the little river which flowed down High Street, into the Lagan. An old map of 1685 shows this small dock, which was cleaned out and deepened as was required. No accommodation for ships or artificial landing-place existed. Some time previous to that, in the year 1613, it was named in the Charter of Belfast as a free port, but small sums were paid by shipmasters. After some extension of the dock had been made, it was enacted in 1696, "That all vessels belonging to foreigners should have liberty to discharge at the 'Key' on payment of twopence a ton, but vessels belonging to Freemen of the Borough should only pay one penny a ton." Gradually the increase of shipping brought increase of harbour dues. In 1775, Lord Avonmore reclaimed part of the causeway across the Strand at Connswater. At a meeting of the harbour corporation held in the Ballast Office in 1786, a resolution was passed, "That the ford opposite Chichester Street is of great detriment to the harbour and shipping, and ought to be removed at once." £10 10s. was allowed for this work, and the stones which were removed were to be sold.

It was found that every year more money was required. In the year 1800, a great advance was made when a new graving-dock was opened to receive vessels. It was capable of containing three vessels of two hundred tons each. At spring tides there were nine feet of water, and it was constructed by the Ballast Corporation at a cost of £6,000.

The Belfast Harbour Commissioners were formed in the year 1854. They have now a very handsome building, and the Harbour Trust is one of the most important public boards we have. It is not within the scope of this small book to touch upon the vast importance of their work.

CHAPTER XIV

SOME OLD COUNTRY HOUSES

There are still to be found about Belfast the remains of some of the old country houses: and we shall find that many have a story attached to them, that comes down to us from the twilight of the shadowy past.

Ballydrain is one of the most interesting. It belonged to—and was probably built by—a family named Stewart. They came from Scotland in the year 1605, and resided for many generations in the house, and they intermarried with many well-known families. The estate was afterwards bought by Mr. Montgomery, whose descendants still live at Ballydrain.[1]

Hospitality was always a striking characteristic of the Irish people, and in the early times people travelled slowly over very bad roads with no light, and there was but poor accommodation for travellers. Inns were a long distance apart, so some benevolent people received travellers and took them into their houses for rest and refreshment. There were many houses of this kind throughout the country. In the year 1675, we find there was a Free House at Ballydrain, where poor travellers could procure food and lodging. A stone is still to be seen, which was built into the wall of the house, with this inscription carved on it.

"A Free House 1675."

One of the Stewart family built Macedon, another built Maryville and Myrtlefield, and also a house called Windsor in the Ballydrain grounds. Maryville on the Malone Road has belonged to the Wilson family for generations. Tradition says it was at Cranmore, beside Maryville, that King William rested when on his way to Belfast, and the tree where his horse was tied is still to be seen. Cranmore was formerly named Orange Grove, and was the residence of a family named Eccles. The jug which King William drank out of and the bed he slept in were for a long time treasured in the house.

Malone House is erected on the site of a very extensive fort, called Castle Cam, or Freeston Castle, but there are no remains of the ancient fort now to be seen. There was also an old Church on the top of the hill in Upper Malone called "Capella de Crookmuck". The trees in the grounds surrounding Malone House are remarkable for their stately beauty and wide-spreading branches. There were several ancient forts in the same neighbourhood, but any history of them cannot now be found. On the left of the road leading to Shaw's Bridge, the foundations of a fort are still seen. There are remains of a third in the grounds near Lismoyne, and yet another was in Friar's Bush graveyard.

Wilmont is also a fine old house; it was built in the year 1740. Purdysburn belonged to the Hill-Wilson family, and was at one time the residence of the Bishop of Down. In the year 1812, it became the property of the well-known Batt family, who built large additions to the house. It now belongs to the Corporation of Belfast, and the beautiful old mansion is used as a Lunatic Asylum[2]. Certainly, if lovely and peaceful surroundings can assist in restoring health and sanity to the mind diseased, such should be found there. Part of the demesne is occupied with the extensive buildings of the Infectious Diseases Hospital, which are in what was once known as the "Fort Field", where there was a very perfect old fort, with trees planted at regular intervals round the moat. In the centre of the fort there is a most curious tree, said to be about eight hundred years old. Perhaps the fort may be opened at some future time; and it would doubtless well repay the trouble of excavation to find a *souterrain*[3] and unexpected treasure still securely hidden under the ancient holy tree which has guarded the secret for so many long years.

The grounds belonging to Purdysburn are more beautiful and picturesque than in any other place about Belfast. The old garden was laid out in the form of the "Union Jack", and the design was carried out with all the borders planted with the colours red, white and blue. The wonderful yew-tree hedges are unequalled in the North of Ireland.

The name of Stranmillis has a pleasant origin. It is Irish, from "Struthan-Milis", a sweet stream. The castle at Stronemellis was built in the year 1612, and many people even yet find it pleasant to walk along the banks of the old sweet stream. There was once an old castle of primitive construction in the grounds of Stranmillis.

Belvoir Park has also a most interesting history. It was once the residence of Lord Dungannon, and there is a very old graveyard inside the grounds, where a vault is still to be seen, the burial place of Viscount Dungannon, but not a vestige now remains of the old church. There is a great oak tree yet standing in the grounds, of such an age, that no one can even guess at it, and the remains of an old fort. But the rosery is still famous for its beauty. The roses bloom and flourish and fling their fragrant breath into the pure air, just as freely as in the days of long ago. The estate passed into Sir Thomas Bateson's possession, and his heir was Lord Deramore.

Annadale Hall and Belvoir Park were at one time all one estate. Lord Dungannon built a wall dividing it, and he also built the wall which encloses the Giant's Ring. Annadale received its name from "Anna", the mother of the Duke of Wellington. She was a daughter of Arthur Hill, of Dungannon, and it is said that the great Duke often visited his mother here. A Colonel Arthur Hill was the founder of the Downshire family, and he was a younger son of the Sir Moyses Hill who built Stranmillis. Lord Donegall also lived at Annadale for some time, and tradition says that Lady Blessington was a resident there, and later on she lived at the house now known as the Queen's Hotel, at the corner of York Street, but tradition is not always to be relied on.

Parkmount, on the Shore Road, was in the year 1666 a lodge or occasional residence of Lord Donegall, and it afterwards passed into possession of Ludfords, Cairns, and McNeills.

Fort William was once a fort seventy feet square, with a deep fosse surrounding it, and it was defended by a bastion at each angle. It was built by William III. in the year 1690.

There was a ruder fort constructed at an earlier date, called Mount Essex. It was built by the Earl of Essex. Abbeylands at Whiteabbey derives its name from the remains of an abbey which was once there, and a few fragments of the old walls are still standing. It was the residence of General Sir Hugh McCalmont Cairns.

Belmont is also a very old place. Mr. Will Bateson bought it in the year 1776. It afterwards became the property of Lord Ranfurley, whose name is still seen on some streets in the neighbourhood. Sir Thomas McClure purchased it, and at his death the old house was taken down, and Campbell College was erected there in the year 1894. It is an ideal place for a public school.

Mount Pottinger takes its name from the old family of Pottinger. Sir Henry Pottinger was a great naval officer, and General Pottinger was also a very famous man. Three members of this family won great renown in India, and Sir Henry in China. The oldest name on a Belfast tombstone is that of a Pottinger in the year 1602, and now, except in history, the name is unknown.

Ormiston was built by Mr. Coombe, and, although not one of the old country mansions, it is noted as the residence of Sir Edward Harland, and after his death it passed into the possession of Lord Pirrie.

Hyde Park, on the Antrim Road, belonged to a well-known Belfast family named Hyde, who had extensive cotton print works there.

The modern residences are now too numerous to be mentioned, but they testify in a remarkable manner to the increasing wealth and prosperity of the city.

CHAPTER XV

THUROT'S INVASION

It makes a pleasant surprise in one's reading to turn over unexpectedly a page of romantic daring, and to find the story of a gallant young hero just at your own door. An Irish officer named Farrel accompanied James II. to France, after the Revolution. His grandson, O'Farrel, or Thurot—as he was afterwards named—was born in France. He was early in life left an orphan, and he suffered many hardships. He lived for some time in England, then came to Dublin, lived in Glenarm and Carlingford, and so was very familiar with all the Northern coast of Ireland.

His knowledge of every port and harbour was so accurate that he was chosen by the French Government as the Commander of a squadron. In the year 1759, Commodore Thurot left France with five frigates to invade Ireland, but his enterprise was unfortunate at the outset. The autumnal equinox met his fleet with such severity that one of the frigates returned to France, another was lost to sight and never heard of again, but the courage of the intrepid Thurot kept the remaining three together, even though the storm blew them into the North Sea, and he was compelled to spend the winter in Norway and the Orkney Islands. When calmer weather came, he set sail for Ireland, and arrived in Lough Foyle early in the new year. He may perhaps have remembered the history of the "Maiden City", for he wisely made no attempt to molest Derry, but he suddenly appeared before Carrickfergus and boldly demanded its surrender. On the 21st of February, he placed himself at the head of his men and attacked the town. Colonel Jennings was in command of the Castle, which did not possess even one mounted cannon, and the garrison numbered only one hundred and fifty men. There was a brave resistance, but the Castle was obliged to surrender, and the French landed and plundered the town, after levying contributions from the wealthy inhabitants. Thurot took three prisoners, who were afterwards recovered on board his ship.

A touching incident occurred when Thurot landed and advanced with his troops through High Street, and the French men drove the English back. A little child, "Thomas", the son of the Sheriff, John Seeds, ran out of the house, and playfully stood between the conflicting parties. The French officer in command lifted the child in his arms and ran to the nearest door with him, which happened to be his father's, and having placed the child in safety, he then advanced at the head of his men. Forcing one of the gates of the Castle, he was the first to enter, and he was killed between the two gates. He was seen to take a picture from his bosom and died kissing it. He belonged to the noble French family of D'Esterre, and was a remarkably handsome man. Great men have often very tender hearts, and the story of D'Esterre's kindly thoughtfulness for a little child lived long in the history of Carrickfergus.

Thurot sent a message to Belfast threatening an attack unless provisions were sent for his men at once. This declaration roused the national spirit of the people, and immense numbers of men poured into Belfast. In twenty-four hours, the town was secure from insult and danger of the French invasion.

A strong barricade was erected at Milewater, and thousands of men armed themselves with weapons, and with Lord Charlemont at the head of his "Defenders", marched to Carrickfergus, while five thousand volunteers remained to protect Belfast. Thurot re-embarked his troops, and his ships were seen lying outside the harbour when Lord Charlemont arrived. The French General Flobert and twenty men were left behind in a wounded condition, and they were afterwards provided with suitable lodgings and assistance. Thurot was met, as he was leaving the Lough, by Captain Elliott, with a squadron of three ships, and, after a sharp action of one hour and a half in the Irish Sea, Thurot was killed and his ships taken into English ports. The French prisoners were brought to Belfast, and kept for three months, when they were sent home in two frigates.

Such a kindly feeling grew on both sides, that great regret was expressed when the time arrived for the Frenchmen to leave. They asked and received permission to give a ball in the Market House as a token of their gratitude for all the kindness shown to them during their stay. Two hundred ladies and gentlemen attended the farewell ball, and it is recorded as being a scene of "brilliant grandeur".

Indeed, some of the Frenchmen remained behind, no longer as prisoners but as honoured inhabitants of Belfast. So ended the invasion of Carrickfergus. Thurot was a brave man, full of high courage and intrepid daring. He possessed great ability and died fighting for his adopted country, and he was the last to surrender on the deck of his ship. Instead of the £50,000 he had proudly demanded as a fine from Belfast, he left his dead body as a memento of his ill-fated expedition.

Thurot's gold watch is in the possession of a gentleman near Belfast. It is still in good order and still keeps time.

The story of Paul Jones has been often told, and he figures in many old American books as a hero of romance. Even his enemies had to acknowledge his unfailing courage and his genius. He was born at Kirkcudbright in Scotland, but from a very early age followed the sea, where he made a notorious reputation as a privateer. His line of life would in these days be called by a different name.[1]

A few years after Thurot's ill-fated attempt on Carrickfergus, there was a revolt in the American Colonies, in which France joined with America, and they were united against England. It was a time of great excitement, and many a stirring tale has been written of that long conflict. In April of the year 1778, the famous Paul Jones suddenly appeared in Belfast Lough, with an armed ship called the *Ranger*.

A ship, the *Draper*, was lying in Garmoyle, laden with a very valuable cargo of linen, and it was thought at first that Jones would attack that ship and take possession of the cargo. But he had more ambitious ideas than to seize a small affair like a load of linen, when a king's ship was within his reach. A sloop of war, the *Drake*, was lying off Carrickfergus. He brought his ship into the Lough to attack the man-of-war, but the weather was unfavourable for making the attempt. Paul Jones never was a man to lose much time, so he turned the *Ranger* about and sailed to Whitehaven, where he spiked the guns[2], burned several ships, and then proceeded to pay a brief but disastrous visit to his native town of Kirkcudbright. He plundered the mansion house of Lord Selkirk, and then returned to Belfast Lough to try and capture the *Drake*, which was still lying in Carrickfergus Roads[3]. The two vessels engaged in battle, and after a few hours of determined conflict the *Ranger* was victorious, and Paul Jones conquered and captured the English man-of-war. He left Belfast Lough with flying colours after two days with as much variety in warfare in them as even he could desire. No one regretted his departure, and no one ever wished for a return visit. This adventure of Paul Jones impressed the people with the fact that our Lough was in a totally defenceless condition. Carrickfergus Castle even at its best days could not protect our shores.

A fort for the defence of Belfast has been built at Grey Point, the guns of which command the entrance to the Lough, and it is now almost completed.[4]

The town of Belfast was seriously alarmed, and applied to the Government for assistance, but none was given, so the people took matters into their own hands and fitted out privateers with men and guns for protection. It was at this time[5] that armed companies of citizens were formed, and they were the first of the famous Volunteers. Men of the highest rank enlisted, and rapid progress was made in preparation for any emergency.

The House of Lords wrote a letter of thanks to the Volunteers, who sought no reward and asked for no payment from the English Government. They took no military oath or obligation, but depended on their own resources, expecting to be engaged in war with France. During the winter they guarded the town and their intrepidity and knowledge protected both town and country from enemies. It would be a very curious sight now if the Volunteers were seen with their picturesque dress, of scarlet coat with black velvet facings, white waistcoats and breeches, going in procession to church on Sunday, and firing three volleys afterwards on the Parade as they returned. The Volunteers were at the beginning of their organisation a most useful and splendid body of men. There was a great Volunteer Convention held at Dungannon in the year 1782.

Annual reviews took place in Belfast, intense enthusiasm prevailed and all doors were open to receive them as honoured guests. The Charitable Society—now the old Poorhouse—gave shelter, and parades were held inside its walls. Reviews were held in the Plains and Falls Meadows for three days, in which thousands took part, with 100,000 spectators. Balls and assemblies were held every night, and Belfast was very brilliant, but dissensions came in, and the United Irishmen were formed. In 1793, the Government caused the Volunteer regiments to be broken up, but during the years of their existence the Volunteers had served the country, and served it well.

CHAPTER XVI

THE CAVE HILL

There have been many stories written and many poems on the beauty of our Cave Hill, but perhaps the finest is by a well-known Belfast writer[1], who has given us these beautiful lines.

> Look up from the streets of the city,
> Look high beyond tower and mast,
> What hand of what Titan sculptor
> Smote the crags on the mountain vast?
> Made when the world was fashioned,
> Meant with the world to last,
> The glorious face of the sleeper
> That slumbers above Belfast.

It is a glorious face indeed, so calm in its majestic beauty, upturned to the blue vault of heaven, as if it scorned the small things of this poor earth of ours.

That wonderful face was there long ages before the Sphinx gazed over the plain of Gizeh, and will be there when all the work of our world is done.

Sometimes when I see the outline of that face clear cut against the sky, I wonder, if those still firm lips could speak, what tales they could tell. If those closed eyes could open what have the centuries to tell us that they do not know? Look at it from every point of view, and still our own Cave Hill stands unrivalled. Ben Madhigan is well named the Hill of Caves, for there are three large caves on the face of the precipice. They were used in the old war times as hiding places for prisoners as well as for treasure. Sir Samuel Ferguson tells us they were also used as hiding places for the people in times of danger. The lowest cave is quite easy of access, and it opens just above the large semi-circle which is called the Devil's Punch Bowl. It is twenty-one feet long, eighteen feet wide, varies from seven to ten feet high, and it is dry and clean. The next cave is ten feet long, seven feet wide and six feet high. The third cave is the largest, but so difficult of access, that few people venture to ascend such a dangerous cliff. It is very extensive and is divided into two parts. It must have been in this upper cave that Corby MacGilmore kept his prisoners.

The secret entrance from the top of the hill remains a secret still, which may some day be discovered. Corby used to show his unfortunate prisoners the open mouth of the cave and tell them they were free to depart by his front door—if they could— but we are not told that any of his unwilling guests ever went out of that door by their own desire. Even the magnificent view outside would but poorly compensate for the imprisonment inside the cave. So recently as the year 1874, two other caves were discovered, and they are larger, but are extremely difficult of access. One of them measures thirty feet by twenty. A strange and unknown name has been cut into the rock. No living person can read the meaning of the name, and the hands that cut it on the stone have crumbled into dust many a long year ago. It leaves, however, another indication that all these caves must at one time have been used.

There are several places about Belfast where large ramparts of earth have been formed, most probably for purposes of defence and protection. Raths and ancient forts are also numerous.

The largest of these is on the lofty summit of the Cave Hill, and is known as MacArt's Fort. The noble face on the hill has often been called the Goddess of Liberty, and MacArt's Fort forms the Phrygian cap that crowns the head. On one side, there is a precipice, and on the other, a single ditch of great depth and a vallum[3] of large dimensions, while the enclosure is almost level. On the highest point, there is a chair formed in the rock, which was used on most important occasions by the Irish chieftains in the dawn of our Irish history.

The last historical event which took place on the top of MacArt's Fort was on a day in June in the year 1795, when Wolfe Tone, Thomas Russell, Samuel Nelson, and several others met and took a solemn oath that they would never rest until Ireland was free. Tragic death came soon to some of their little band. All are at rest long since, but Ireland will never rest.

The Cave Hill used to be a popular resort for holiday makers, and it is still a favourite walk. The path has been made much easier now, and the toil of the ascent is forgotten when the top is reached and the wide-spreading panorama of beautiful scenery lies at the foot. It is quite possible that in the near future the ascent may be made in a much less laborious fashion, if we have the Belfast City Tramway service extended to MacArt's Fort. The beautiful face of the Goddess of Liberty will, we hope, still slumber undisturbed in her majestic dignity.

The Caves of Ben Madhigan are not the only caves we have about Belfast. These curious relics of antiquity are to be found in various places formed in the earth or of hard limestone. In the year 1792, three were discovered at Wolfhill. One is eight yards long but only one yard wide, and it has four small chambers diverging from it. On the side of the hill at Ballymargy is another cave larger and more perfect, with two entrances.

A very large cave near Hannahstown has been closed since 1798. It was formerly used for concealing arms. In the same neighbourhood at a place called Callender's Fort, two miles from Belfast on the Falls Road, is another ancient place named "Cranock" where traces of foundations and the remains of a large cemetery are still left. On the same road is the old chapel of Kilwee, where a number of finely carved crosses and monuments were found.

Two cairns were discovered on the Black Mountain in the year 1827. One was remarkable, as it contained a large urn filled with human bones, with a spear-head and two brass ornaments. There is also a cairn on the Cave Hill and one at Squire's Hill. At the base of Squire's Hill, there are two small raths, and also two larger ones near the summit of the Black Mountain.

Mention has already been made of an encampment at Fort William which was made by King William in the year 1690, near the site of a ruder and much older construction. There was another very ancient fortress, three miles along the road to Carrickfergus at Greencastle, but we have no distinct record of it extant now.

CHAPTER XVII

EARLY INDUSTRIES

Paper-making, printing and book-binding are all very old industries in Belfast, and are still an important part of the trade of the town. The progress which has taken place has been most remarkable. Paper-making was carried on at Antrim and at Randalstown by Francis Joy. It is now manufactured at Ballyclare, where there are extensive paper-mills[1], and a large number of people are employed. In 1749, Francis Joy received a grant of £200 from Parliament for improvements, and he introduced the first machinery in the North of Ireland for making paper. His mills at Antrim were erected in 1776, but they were burnt down and then rebuilt. A man named McManus, who had lived in France, came to Ireland about that time. He settled in Dunmurry and introduced paper-making there. Mr. Henry Joy had the old paper-mill which was worked by the water of the Blackstaff river. It occupied the ground between Joy Street and where the Gas Office now is in Ormeau Avenue, but not a vestige of it remains at the present time. In the year 1803, he advertised that he had removed his place of business to Pottinger's Entry, where all kinds of paper suitable for shops could be had.

When Henry Joy used his water wheel at Blackstaff River, there was only one other water wheel in Belfast, which was of a much older date, and was in a corn mill. It was at the old

Manor Mill in the days of Queen Elizabeth[2], and later on it was used to grind the meal for the Parliamentary troops in the seventeenth century.

Shane O'Neill had the first printing-press in Ireland. He kept it in Shane's Castle, and used it there. The first printing-press in Belfast belonged to Mr. James Blow in the year 1690. A Bible is still in existence which bears the date of 1702, "printed by James Blow."

His original wooden printing-press was used in Youghal until the year 1824. A very beautiful little book, which is also still to be seen, was printed by Patrick Neill & Co. in 1700. It is "The Psalms of David in Meeter" and each page is four inches in length by two and a quarter in breadth. On the first page is written, "David Smith's gift to Belfast Meeting House, 1705." It was beautifully bound in tortoise-shell, and the back, hinges, corners and ornaments were made of solid silver. Mr. David Smith was at that time Sovereign of the town.

When John Wesley preached in Belfast in 1789, he was welcomed at the First Presbyterian Meeting House and had a very crowded service in the morning, but he was not allowed to hold a second service, as some sinner had stolen the silver rims and clasp off the Bible, but the "Psalm Book" was left undamaged.

The *Belfast Newsletter* was the first newspaper in Belfast. It was printed at the sign of the "Peacock" in Bridge Street in the year 1737, and the paper used was made in Joy's Mill in Randalstown.

It was printed twice a week at first, but in 1855 became a daily paper. It was the custom long ago for the newspapers to be carried about and left at houses and offices at a charge of one penny for an hour, but that must have been in very early days indeed, and wonderful changes have taken place in the newspapers since then. For a great many years every newspaper was obliged to pay a tax of one penny on each copy, which was marked on the paper with a large red stamp, but this tax was removed later on.

The old Almanacks of Belfast are very interesting. There was one made for the use of the Earl of Donegall in the year 1666. Another in 1678 was a most valuable and curious production. It was two-and-a-half inches long and was bound in shagreen[3] with handsome silver clasps.

"Poor Robin's Almanack" was published by H. and R. Joy in 1753, and it continued for many years, and was always held in high estimation. In the Belfast and County Almanack for the year 1770, the following words are used:

> You'll find this neat and useful book,
> And yearly Trav'ler true as watch or clock,
> Though small in form great matter comprehends,
> Well known to all its patron friends.

There were many other industries in Belfast from very early times. Leather was an old and important trade and tanning was extensively carried on. Vitriol works[4] were also successful.

Sugar refining was in Sugar House Entry. Foundry and iron works were established at an early date.

The largest glass works were at Carrick Hill, where pottery, glass and china were manufactured, cut and engraved flint glass being a special production, but the place was sold out in 1809.

There was a well-known industry at Lambeg for woollen goods.

Blankets were sold from 18*s.* up to £6 6*s.*, stockings were also made at the same place and had a high reputation. Soap and candle making were also well known and both are still carried on extensively.

Brewing beer and whisky are old industries, as whisky[5] has been made in Ireland since the year 1460, and there are now large distilleries in Belfast.

The manufacture of mineral waters is a very large and important trade, but it would be quite impossible to mention all the great and growing industries of the city.

Business and the progressive methods of conducting business affairs have undergone such changes, that it is curious to look back to the easygoing old days and to realise that the Belfast of to-day is the place where life once ran on such peaceful lines as we read of in such notices as these. A little bookshop at the corner of North Street and Rosemary Street used to be closed now and then, and a card put up in the window with "Gone to Dublin, will be back in a few days." And it was quite customary on a fine day in July to see a notice displayed on the closed shutters of many shops with the intimation "Gone to the Races." No one was ever surprised at this method of business and the customers had to wait until the races were over.

In 1822, three weeks frequently elapsed between the time of the steamboat's arrival from Liverpool, for there was no undue haste in those happy times, and on the whole, people got on perhaps just as well.

The rate of living at the high pressure of the twentieth century does not tend either to longer life or happier days.

If we take a map of the world and look closely at it, we shall find Ireland a very small place indeed, and Belfast is not even marked on it. Then take a map of Ireland and we see our city is just a little dot, not very much to look at, but this Belfast of ours possesses four of the biggest things in the world and we may well be proud of our city. It is a curious fact that this small country is known all over the world for four great industries.

Messrs. Gallaher's tobacco factory in York Street, Belfast, is the largest manufactory of its kind in the world. The immense building covers four acres of ground and is six stories high. Raw tobacco is sent here, from every country where tobacco grows, to be manipulated and sent back again in many different forms. It gives employment to a great number of people. All over the world Gallaher's tobacco is known.

We must now go back to earlier times. Sir Walter Raleigh brought tobacco and potatoes into Great Britain in the year 1585. But we find the custom of smoking is of much greater antiquity in Ireland than the introduction of tobacco into Europe. Bronze smoking pipes are frequently found in our Irish tumuli or sepulchral mounds of great antiquity. Similar pipes made of baked clay have been discovered in all parts of the island.

A great battle took place in the tenth century between the Irish and the Danes. Long afterwards among the human bones left on the scene of the battle, many pipes were found. Crofton Croker writes that in the year 1784, in Brannockstown, in Kildare, amongst some remains, an ancient tobacco pipe was found sticking between the teeth of a human skull. Surely that man must have met with a sudden death! Crofton Croker had a great collection of pipes found in the ground about Limerick, Cork and Dublin.

A most curious instance which proves the antiquity of smoking is found in Corcumroe Abbey in County Clare. There is a recumbent figure on a monument erected to the memory of Donogh O'Brien, King of Thomond, who was killed in the year 1227 and was buried in the Abbey, which was founded by his family. He is represented lying in the usual position with the short pipe or "dudeen" of the Irish in his mouth. It is a very realistic piece of sculpture.

Some of the old pipes are very small. They are called "fairy pipes" and there is a most interesting collection of them exhibited in the Science and Art Museum in Dublin. We do not know what was used by the smokers of long ago, but we may suppose that they used some kind of dried herbs, which must have been a powerful mixture. This would also explain why the pipes were made so small.

Among the early records of Belfast we find in the year 1782 there is a tobacco industry mentioned. There were thirty-eight tobacco spinners giving employment to 152 children. During the next ten years every trade had increased except tobacco, and owing to the revenue laws, the trade fell so low that employment was given to only twenty children. Now, in Gallaher's factory alone, the fragrant weed gives constant employment to over 2,000 employees. It is one of the four greatest industrial concerns in the world, and is likely to increase as more tobacco is grown in Ireland. The Customs duty paid yearly is about one million and a quarter. Another factory quite as large is in Virginia. It also belongs to Messrs. Gallaher.

CHAPTER XVIII

ROPE-MAKING

The Belfast Ropeworks Company is known over the world, not only as being the largest in existence, but also for the variety and excellence of its products. It now covers an extent of thirty-four acres, and gives employment to many thousands. Until the year 1740, all cordage was imported from England, then a ropemaking place was commenced by John McCracken in the year 1758.

John Street was in 1800 known as the old Rope Walk. This street was absorbed in Royal Avenue, and was swept away when the new thoroughfare was opened. Thomas Ekenhead was for many years the principal ropemaker in Belfast. His private residence is now a bonded store in Donegall Quay. It was once considered to be a very fine house, and at that time was at the edge of the river, with a lovely prospect of green fields and trees, and an uninterrupted view as far as the Holywood hills. Thomas Ekenhead died of cholera in 1832. His brother, Captain Ekenhead, swam across the Hellespont with Lord Byron, which is mentioned in "Hero and Leander"[1] in the lines where he tells of the reckless lover who swam across the dividing waters. "Leander, Mr. Ekenhead and I did." Their sister Mrs. Dummitt, built and endowed the Ekenhead Church in memory of her brother Thomas. She also founded a scholarship in Trinity College for lads from County Down.

Then in later years we find the Belfast Ropeworks Company

has made a marvellous business. Every kind of rope and cord that is possible, from the heaviest cable to the finest twine, is made here. Another most interesting branch of the work is making fishing nets, which have to be made by hand. The firm turns out one hundred tons of rope and twine every week, and gives employment to 3,600 workers. When visiting the place the machines for winding the cord into balls are well worth special attention, as it is done so quickly and neatly, and all the work is finished in the most perfect manner.

CHAPTER XIX

LINEN

The next greatest manufactory in the world is the linen industry of York Street Mill. Perhaps we might go back to the very earliest history of linen, and trace its wonderful increase and vast improvement up to the present time. The manufacture of linen began in the East. The Phoenicians planted colonies in Carthage and Spain and from thence it came to Ireland, and with it the spindle and loom. The very earliest English writers speak of Irish linen as an essential part of dress. In early ages, the Irish wore long linen garments dyed yellow, the dye being made from lichen.

The first notice of Irish linen in England was in the time of Henry III., 1272. Henry VIII. mentioned that Irish linen had been exported for one hundred years. In his time, the Irish used linen in extravagant quantities, thirty yards being put into one garment. Queen Elizabeth passed a bill to forbid steeping the flax in water, which proves to us now, that although she knew a great many things, there were still a few she did not know. She passed another law to forbid more than seven yards of linen to be used for one shirt. In the year 1698, the woollen trade of Ireland was so successful that the English were seriously displeased about it, and some most unjust laws were passed to prohibit the woollen manufacture.

In the year 1702, Mr. Lewis Cromelin came to Lisburn and

brought 1,000 looms from Holland, and a number of improved spinning wheels. Manufacturers used to bleach their own linen, but as time went on it was sent out to be bleached, and this became a special branch of the linen trade.

Up to the year 1770, linen was bleached with buttermilk, and nothing else was used. At Malone no buttermilk could be bought, as it all went to the bleach greens.

From 1781, all linen was computed at 1s. 4d., which was changed later. Lawn was 5s. a yard, and cambric £1 2s. 9d. unbleached.

Then diaper and damask were made. John Holden made diaper in the year 1730, and it is wonderful to trace the development of the industry as it improves step by step. William Coulson commenced a damask factory at Lisburn in 1766, which continues to make the finest quality. Another at Ardoyne was opened in the year 1825, and both of these places are celebrated for the superior excellence of their damask.

The linen industry steadily increased until it became necessary to open a central hall for the convenience of the business. The first Linen Hall was in Ann Street, in 1739. Lord Donegall gave £1,500 towards building it. The next was in Donegall Street where St. Anne's Church was afterwards built. It was after some time removed to a building on the other side of the street, where the date may still be seen cut over the doorway, "Brown Linen Hall, 1773." A stranger passing along the street, who might pause to look through the doorway, might very well be excused for thinking it was a neglected graveyard. The old stone tables where the goods were exhibited for sale are almost hidden beneath a luxuriant crop of tall grass and weeds.

An ancient lawsuit has at last been settled touching a claim against the place. A man came from Maghera in County Derry every Friday with a web of brown linen, which he opened on one of the old stone tables. He said that as long as it was exposed for sale the Brown Linen Hall could not be closed.

For forty-three years, through summer sunshine and winter snow, he never missed a Friday, and at his death his son carried on the old custom, but the place is now utterly deserted, roofless and broken down. Fortunately the brown linen trade was not all buried there.

The White Linen Hall was built in the year 1787, and Lord Donegall with his usual generosity gave the four acres of ground on which it was built. The place was then known as the Castle Meadows. It stood at that time alone in a quiet spot, and afterwards the fine old houses in Donegall Square were built. Many people still remember the pleasant garden and shady trees which surrounded the old Linen Hall. Modern improvements have now swept it away, and the City Hall stands in its place. There was a line of old trees and gardens fronting the Linen Hall from Chichester Street on to Fountain Street. It is really not so very long ago since bluebells and primroses were growing where stately buildings now stand at each corner of Donegall Square. But we must come back to the largest factory in the world. York Street Mill is an enormous place with additional works in Henry Street, York Road and Antrim. It gives constant employment to many thousands. It has 90,000 spindles and 1,000 power looms, and is indeed a busy hive of industry.

In the year 1900, there were 900,000 spindles running in

Belfast alone, more than in any country in the world. Ulster has more than any three countries combined. There are 35,000 power looms in Ulster and 22,000 in Great Britain and the Continent of Europe combined.

CHAPTER XX

SHIPBUILDING

When Queen Elizabeth received her first report of Belfast from her Lord Deputy in the year 1538, he mentioned that it seemed a very suitable place for shipbuilding, and many people think so still. In 1663, small vessels were built in or near Belfast, vessels from six to twelve tons and manned by two or three men.

A great and exceptional effort was made a few years before that time. When the Presbyterians were persecuted and ordered to leave the country in the year 1636, a ship was built for them of 150 tons. It sailed for America, but was driven back by adverse winds and *The Eagle's Wing* was obliged to land her passengers in Scotland. We next read of a great stride in shipbuilding, when the *Loyal Charles* of 250 tons was built and launched. Shipbuilding was almost dead when William Ritchie arrived in Belfast. He improved matters very much, and saved both time and expense by repairing vessels here, for formerly they had to be sent away. He visited Belfast in March, 1791, and returned in July of the same year. Ritchie had quickly grasped the future possibilities of shipbuilding in Belfast, so he gave up the yard in Saltcoats and began work here. He brought ten men, apparatus and materials. His brother was an apprentice, and received one third of the business profits until 1793 when they dissolved partnership. He died in 1807, but his work was continued by another brother, John.

William built ships from 50 to 450 tons burden, and John was also successful. There were only six jobbing ship-carpenters in Belfast when he came here. There was no head to direct them, and they had frequently long spells of idleness. Vessels were built and repaired in England and Scotland, but William Ritchie brought with him joiners, blockmakers and blacksmiths. The best work was done in his own shop. He cast anchors of all sizes up to 14 *cwt*[1]. He did a wonderfully progressive work, he reclaimed land from the sea, embanked it and fronted the quays with stone for his own shipyard, and his graving dock held three vessels of 200 tons. He paid in wages £120 a week, considered a large sum in those days. He engaged to build a dock for the Ballast Office, which occupied four years and was finished in the year 1800. It was known as Ritchie's Dock for many years. His ships for the West Indies and for trading were built of oak, and it was said that "for elegance of mould, fastness of sailing, and utility in every respect they are unrivalled in any of the ports they trade to." This was written of the Belfast-built ships in the year 1811, and the same words might be used again in the year 1913.

Ritchie and McLaine introduced steam navigation, and they built the first steamship in Ireland. William Ritchie retired from business ten years before his death. His shipyard was beside the Harbour Office, and a remnant of the old smithy still exists at the entrance to the tile yard of Messrs. W. D. Henderson & Co., between the Harbour Office and the graving docks.

His business was afterwards carried on by Charles Connell & Sons. The last survivor of this firm—Alexander—was well known, and is still remembered as a great sportsman. Alexander McLaine, who was also a Scotchman, married a daughter of John Ritchie, and the firm was carried on as Ritchie & McLaine, and later on as Alexander McLaine & Sons. This firm existed until the year 1879. The family of McLaine was well known, and most highly respected in Belfast for a great number of years.

The first steamship that was seen in Belfast was a Scotch boat called the *Rob Roy*, and she excited great curiosity in the year 1819 when she plied between Belfast and Glasgow. Ritchie built the *Chieftain* and the engines were made in the Lagan Foundry. It was built for George Langtry, a member of a well-known Belfast family, and it was used as a passenger boat to Liverpool in 1826. Another, the *Erin*, had the unheard-of audacity of attempting to go to London, and actually ventured on the hazardous journey, but alas! for good intentions, she was lost at the Isle of Man. The first iron boat was built in 1838, which was a wonderful step from the wooden ships. She was built in the yard of the Lagan Foundry. In the same year Ireland had the honour of sending out the first steamboat that ever crossed the Atlantic Ocean. She was owned by the City of Dublin Steamship Company. The *Royal William* crossed to America in nineteen days, and returned in fourteen and a half. There was a scene of the wildest excitement when the *Royal William* left the quay in Liverpool. Thousands of people lined the pier to see the venturesome vessel set out on her perilous voyage. The enthusiasm was unbounded, and she left the Mersey amid frantic excitement, loud cheering and cannon firing at many points.

In the year 1853, part of the Queen's Island was taken

by Robert Hickson & Company for a shipbuilding yard, the beginning of that work on the County Down side of the river. We may here say a word about the Queen's Island. It was formed of slob-land which was thrown up when the new channel was formed under the superintendence of the engineer, Mr. William Dargan. For many years it was known as "Dargan's Island", but after Queen Victoria's visit to Belfast in 1849, the name was changed to the "Queen's Island". It was the first People's Park, and was for a great number of years a fine outlet for holiday makers. There was a large glass building, resembling a miniature Crystal Palace, containing a winter garden and a small Zoo. The outside gardens were very well planted, and tastefully arranged. A long row of bathing boxes occupied one side of the Island, and they were used by many people. It was a pleasant holiday resort, and was open to all who paid one halfpenny to be ferried across the river, so the outing combined the excitement of a sea voyage with a rest afterwards on one of the seats under the pleasant shade of the trees. At the North end, there was a battery with cannon mounted, which were used on very special occasions of public rejoicing, until on one hapless day one of them burst, and so the salutes were stopped. Except the name and the memory, nothing now remains of the once well-known pleasure grounds.

In the year 1859, Mr. E. J. Harland came to Belfast, and he changed the map. Mr. G. W. Wolff joined him in 1861, and since then their success has simply been a world's wonder. It is amusing to look back and remember now that, in those early days when these two young men first entertained the idea of shipbuilding, they went to Liverpool to look for land. The Harbour authorities there received their overtures very coldly, considering that they were too young for such a serious undertaking. We must really pardon the Liverpool Harbour Board for such a very natural mistake, as they were then both in their early twenties. So they returned to Belfast, and it is highly probable that the Liverpool authorities may have lived to regret their mistake. However, their loss was most assuredly Belfast's gain. They at first employed 150 men in the year 1861, and built one ship at a time. Now, fifty years after, 14,500 men have constant employment, and their wages bill is £23,000 every week. The largest ships in the world are built and launched here, and the last two cost three millions.

The *Titanic* and *Olympic* were marvellous creations. It was a tremendous stride in fifty years to send out a vessel of 45,000 tons, and the *Olympic*'s anchor alone weighs forty tons.

Sir Edward Harland's statue[2] adorns the front of the City Hall, a handsome alert figure and a striking likeness of one of the finest citizens we ever had.

In 1879, Workman and Clark commenced shipbuilding on the County Antrim side of the river, and they also have been wonderfully successful, and their turn-out of work in the year runs the Queen's Island very close indeed. There has been recently added to Harland and Wolff's a great engineering work in the new gantries, the largest in the world. They are so immense in height and size that they are visible for miles. One cost £120,000 and the other £80,000.

The latest electric floating crane is a wonderful piece of mechanism, for it can lift 250 tons with as much ease as a schoolboy lifts an apple. The yards and workshops cover an extent of eighty acres, and every department is full of interest. In the other three great industries, women find employment, thus not leaving the labouring oar entirely in one hand, but in the Queen's Island there is no room for any work but men's.

What would all these men do if we had not the largest and finest ships in the world to carry our produce to the remotest parts of the earth? So these four immense industries are really blended together, and our Belfast tobacco, ropes and linen cross the seas in our swift-sure Belfast ships, carrying our commerce all the wide world over. What would some of the early pioneers think or say if they could revisit Belfast as it is to-day? Imagine William Ritchie standing on the Alexandra Dock, and looking at the *Olympic*. His feelings might be too deep for words, but his thoughts would be worth recording. After all, perhaps it is as well the early pioneers sleep well where the busy whirr of the looms and clanging of the hammers cannot disturb their well-earned rest. Their work and their names are held in honoured remembrance.

CHAPTER XXI

COTTON

The first piece of cotton woven in Ireland was made by an ancestor of Mr. Francis McCracken in the year 1777. Cotton manufacturing was once a very flourishing and important industry, but has now grievously declined here. When Robert Joy was travelling through North Britain, he was deeply impressed with the cotton industry as a source of opulence in that country.

He was prompted by an earnest desire to serve the working poor of Belfast, and also to improve the more intricate branches of manufacture. After much thought he and Thomas McCabe suggested that spinning cotton yarn might be made a suitable employment for the children in the Poorhouse. They set them to work with common wheels. The first machine was invented by David Manson. Then, finding superior machines were used in England, they introduced them here. A Mr. Nicholas Grimshaw, who had come from England to settle in Belfast, superintended the making of the first spinning machine at Mr. Joy's sole expense. He also brought over an experienced Scotchman to instruct the children in the Poorhouse. Later on he introduced a carding machine. Cotton thread, yarn, candle wick, gloves and stockings were all made by the children in the Poorhouse. In vain Mr. Joy sought pecuniary aid, as he had done so much at his own expense. He then offered the machinery to the Poorhouse, but the trustees refused to accept it, and the reason of their refusal was never made very clear.

Joy, McCabe and McCracken formed a company, and their cotton dimity and Marseilles quilting attained a great celebrity. The first cotton mill was in Francis Street, off Smithfield. It belonged to Captain John McCracken, and his eldest son had a sailcloth factory, and a rope walk in James Street. Another brother had a cotton mill in Donegall Street. Their mother manufactured cambric and bleached it in the Basin Field in Millfield. Mary McCracken, the dearly beloved sister of Henry Joy MacCracken, had a muslin factory in High Street. Their brother-in-law had a cotton mill at Clonard. The first mill to spin by water was erected by Nicholas Grimshaw in the year 1781.

Twenty-three years afterwards, 27,000 people were employed in the cotton mills.

There was a cotton mill in Waring Street, which was worked by a horse in 1796, and another in Millfield. The first steam-engine used in Belfast was at Springfield cotton mill—"Stevenson's". It was used for pumping water to drive a water wheel. The cotton trade was held supreme, and was a most flourishing industry until about the year 1800, when the American war stopped the supply of raw cotton. There were forty-six firms engaged in the trade. Steam-engines were very rare at that time, but there was one that worked a little cotton mill in Cotton Court, and the beam was made of wood.

One factory advertised that their engine would work three days in the week, and would be open to public inspection.

Thomas and Andrew Mulholland were weavers of cotton and

manufacturers of muslin until their mill in York Street was burned in the year 1828. When rebuilding, they had careful inquiry and deliberation whether to prepare for linen or wool. Finally they decided on linen. Afterwards a great number of mills changed to linen work. Lepper's mill was burned in 1875, and Springfield was then the only cotton mill left in Belfast, and perhaps in the whole of Ireland.

Looking back to the early history of the cotton trade, we can scarcely realise how much we are indebted to those men, who in the face of much apathy and indeed active opposition at one time, gave their time, talents and money to establish an industry that brought employment to the working people.

Robert Joy belonged to a well-known Belfast family. They were of Huguenot descent, their name being originally Joyeuse. His ancestor was Francis Joy, who had the first paper mill at Randalstown, and it was he who established the *Belfast Newsletter* in 1737, the third paper in Ireland. His grandson was the ill-fated Henry Joy McCracken, and his son was Lord Chief Baron Joy. Thomas McCabe and McCracken with Nicholas Grimshaw deserve to be most gratefully held in honoured remembrance for their unselfish services to the town. Their names are almost forgotten, and there are few descendants here now. The Grimshaws were mill-owners at Whitehouse and large employers of labour. One Easter Monday, forty members of this family were present at an entertainment on the Cave Hill, and to-day there is not one of the name in or near Whitehouse. Belfast owes a large debt to these pioneers of industry.

CHAPTER XXII

ARMAGH

Belfast cannot claim to be counted as belonging to the olden times. It is a very modern place in comparison with some of the towns near us, but it may perhaps be that very fact that partly makes our city what it is to-day. It sometimes may be that a place of older name and fame is quite content to rest upon that ancient glory, and to consider that the halo of the past will linger over it for ever, and therefore there is no occasion for modern improvement. In this twentieth century the haloes of the past wear thin, and decay may set in, and glorious tradition may not prove enough to flourish on. At the same time we cling to the memories of our former greatness, and in their innermost consciousness, the old inhabitants of our neighbouring towns consider many of Belfast's innovations perhaps—well, just a little vulgar and presumptuous; but when old and modern are alike satisfied with the existing state of affairs, then all is well.

I remember one ancient town where the inhabitants sternly refused to allow one plate-glass window in any shop front, and where the street lamps were only lighted when some special entertainment was taking place. On all other nights, gay and frivolous folk were obliged to wend their way homewards after dark in a very dim religious light.

Henry Kirke White[1] must have been thinking of Ireland

when he wrote:

> Where are the heroes of the mighty past?
> Where the brave chieftains, where the mighty ones
> Who flourished in the infancy of days?
> All to the grave gone down.

Ireland had heroes of fighting fame great and many, but our country was known all over Europe as the home of learning and cultivation of the fine arts. Historians say that for centuries Ireland was the university for Europe. Camden says, "The Saxons flocked from all quarters to Ireland, which was a mart of literature." It is recorded as a mark of respect to many great men, "He was sent to Ireland to be educated." Julius Caesar said "Go to Ireland for information", and this is the testimony of very many famous historians. There were four of the most famous colleges or schools of learning in the North. One of these was at Armagh, one in Newry, one in Bangor, and another in Downpatrick. We shall take Armagh first, as it is still the most important. It is a small place to have so great a history. It figures early and prominently in the most ancient literature of the country. It claims to have been the metropolis and head of the kingdom, as it certainly was the capital of Ulster, from 353 years before the Christian era. Ard Macha was the high place where the kings of Ulster were crowned for hundreds of years. The first Queen Ardmacha lived 1,000 B.C. Queen Macha of the golden hair, who built the great palace of Emania, was killed in battle with three hundred of her men, 350 B.C. The palace and fortress covered twelve acres, now known as Navan Fort, one mile west of the city. Armagh was the centre and battle-ground of numberless conflicts. It was plundered and laid waste many times, and seventeen times it was burned.

St. Patrick resided in Armagh for nine years. and made it the primatial city. He founded the cathedral in the year 445. It was burnt down three times, but was always rebuilt. There was also a monastery near his own house, and attached to it was the famous College which became one of the most celebrated seminaries in Europe, and sent out learned men to diffuse knowledge throughout the civilised world; 7,000 students were studying there at one time. In the year 1162, it was decreed at a synod of Ulster that no one should lecture publicly on theology except such as had studied in Armagh. In the year 1170, the same synod in Armagh passed a decree that redounds to the honour of our country, and it is a fact that is not so widely known as it ought to be. The Primate and bishops assembled, said, "Freedom was God's best gift to man, and no one had a right to hold his fellow man in bondage," and every slave in Ireland was set free.

Ireland was the first country in the civilised world to set the example, and from the year 1170, no slave was kept in Ireland. In the year 1832 Wilberforce brought his bill into Parliament for England to free her slaves, and his bill became law in the year 1836. Long centuries had elapsed after Irish slaves were freed until the same law was passed in England, and we read of auction sales when fifty men and fifty women were sold in the market-place in Hull. In Ireland we may well be proud that we possess a cleaner record.

The Cathedral has been rebuilt, and added to by successive primates, and is full of interest. It is on the site of an older church, and the crypt is still to be seen. An ancient figure of the patron saint with his crozier was found in a compartment surmounted with shamrocks, which is the earliest existing record of our national emblem, and also a figure of St. Peter with his keys and surmounted by a cock was discovered in the wall. There were three friaries and two convents in Armagh and many ancient churches, in one of which St. Lupita, Patrick's sister, was buried. A monastery dedicated to St. Peter and St. Paul furnished part of the building material for one of the Presbyterian churches. The Roman Catholic Cathedral crowns the summit of another hill, and it is a very stately edifice standing in a beautiful situation. A former Primate, Dr. Robinson, was a great benefactor to the city, for he erected the Library, the Palace, the College and many fine and useful buildings. But his name will always be associated with the Observatory, Museum, and astronomical instruments. A medal struck in honour of Dr. Robinson bears this most appropriate inscription, "The Heavens declare the glory of God", and the same words are also cut on the front of the building. The present Royal School of Armagh still keeps up the old tradition of learning and culture for which the city was famous. It was founded in 1627 by Charles I.

The history of the fair city of Armagh is full of intense interest, and it was here the great hall of "Craobh Ruadh" was built, where the order of knighthood was established. The Knights of the Red Branch were the finest body of men who ever lived in Ireland. A townland is still called "Creeve Roe" and the adjoining moat is known as the King's Stables. Indeed we may most truly say that "Over all the land lie crumbling graves."

King Alfred the Great wrote a poem in the year 685, which can be seen in the British Museum. He was educated in the school at Newry and visited Armagh before returning to England. He mentions the beauty of the great church built by St. Patrick.

We may give one verse as it is translated by O'Donovan:

> I found in Armagh the splendid,
> Meekness, wisdom, circumspection,
> Fasting in obedience to the Son of God,
> Noble prosperous sages.

Archbishop Reeves tells us that "no city is so rich in historical associations and yet has so little to show, and so little to tell in the present day." He says St. Patrick's first church is now represented by the Bank of Ireland. The Provincial Bank come closest to St. Columba's and St. Bride's shares its honours with a paddock. St. Peter and St. Paul's afford stabling and garden produce to a modern "rus in urbe"[2] and St. Mary's is lost in a dwelling house. Few writers have more authority than he, and none knew more about Armagh. For five hundred years the city was plundered and burned, and it was rebuilt again and again, so we need not wonder that much of its ancient glory was lost. Enough still remains to make the primatial city a place full of memories and a place to be proud of.

It was a sad day for Ireland when Brian Boru and his son were buried in the Cathedral in the year 1004. They lay in state surrounded by some of their dead warriors for twelve days. Armagh suffered its worst damage from Shane O'Neill in 1566.

Some wonderfully beautiful mementoes of the learning and sanctity of the olden times are still preserved. The "Book of Armagh", a Latin MS. of the New Testament, with Memoirs of St. Patrick, written in the year 807, with its splendidly embossed leather satchel is in the library of Trinity College in Dublin. The "Bell of Armagh" which is believed to have belonged to St. Patrick is in the Royal Irish Academy. Its costly and beautiful shrine was made in 1091.

In the year 1721, Primate Lindsay presented a peal of six bells to the Cathedral. These were said to be among the most melodious in the Empire.

On the first was engraved "1721. When we do ring I sweetly sing." On the second "1721." On the third "Peace and good neighbourhood." On the fourth "God preserves the Church." On the fifth "Abraham Rudhall of the city of Gloucester bell-founder." On the sixth "Ded. R. Tho. Lindsay, Pr. Div. Archiep. Arm. Tot. Hib. Pr. and Metr. 1721."

The "Font" in the Cathedral is a facsimile of the original one which is now in the British Museum.

One of the most beautiful views that could be imagined is the scene from the Church Walk at St. Mark's. Time's effacing finger has swept away many of the ancient landmarks, but the lapse of years only deepens the charm of the primatial city.

It is a place on which memory loves to linger, the magnificent trees, the old city slumbering at one's feet, the blue encircling hills, the Royal School with its garden, famous even in that country of beautiful gardens, the Deanery, the Observatory on Knockbuy Hill, the "Yellow Hill" covered once with buttercups, and Knockmeala, the "Hill of Honey" where so many wild bees are found. The old Palace grounds with Lady Anne's Walk and the two Cathedrals high over all, stand like guardian angels crowning the distant heights.

The winding river gleams through the trees, the golden sunshine and singing birds complete the sweet remembrance and the vivid picture still lives.

CHAPTER XXIII

DUNGANNON

Dungannon was once a place of great importance, and was celebrated as being the ancient stronghold of the O'Neills. Part of the old castle is still in existence, but it experienced the usual vicissitudes of those turbulent ages, and its story is of siege and assault. It was destroyed and rebuilt over and over again.

The O'Neills clung tenaciously to their ancient patrimony. It was their principal place of residence for hundreds of years, and the history of their family is interwoven with Dungannon from the earliest ages. Conn O'Neill built a small Franciscan Monastery on the south side of the town.

The inauguration stone where the O'Neills were crowned as Kings of Ulster, was on the rath of Tullahogue. The last inauguration was in September, 1595, when Hugh O'Neill was crowned. Lord Mountjoy broke it down in the year 1602, and the broken stones were found many years afterwards in a neighbouring orchard. James II. garrisoned the town in 1689, and his troops occupied the castle and remained in Dungannon during that great struggle. Nothing of very much importance occurred until the memorable Volunteer Convention of later years.

The remains of some old monastic ruins and a beautiful cross are still at Donaghmore beside Dungannon.

The Royal School was founded by Charles I. about 1628.

The Primate of Armagh, Dr. Robinson, who did so much for the city of Armagh, extended his generosity to Dungannon, and he erected the present College. He also purchased nine acres and presented the grounds for a building site. The school has a rich endowment of land and money.

The Dungannon of to-day is a busy, prosperous place, and the inhabitants have now a much happier existence than when their forefathers lived under the shadow of a great name and lived too in the pages of history.

> Rain wears away the rock,
> And time has worn away the tribe
> That stood the battle's shock.[1]

James I. gave a charter to Dungannon in which these words occur:

"Two honest, sober and discreet men are to be sent to parliament."

CHAPTER XXIV

ANTRIM

One can scarcely believe that the small, quiet town of Antrim once played a very important part in history. Like many other places, it counts its history back to the days of St. Patrick. He must have had an uncommonly busy time if he really founded all the churches and monasteries for which he is given credit. There is no doubt that there was an abbey in Antrim in very remote times. It is said to have been beside where the "Steeple" or round tower is, which is now one of the principal objects of interest about Antrim. In recent years some excavations were made in the vicinity of the tower, and the foundations of the ancient walls were discovered and a large quantity of human bones. Probably there was a graveyard beside it. The "Round Tower" of Antrim is considered to be one of the most perfect in Ireland, and it is certainly a very striking feature in the neighbourhood. As St. Patrick is said to have been the founder of most of our ancient religious houses, so the "Goban Saor"[1] is credited with the building of many of the fortresses and round towers.

Legend tells that it was the Goban Saor who built the "Round Tower" at Antrim in the seventh century. It is not a matter of much importance now who built it, but whoever he was, he built, not for a brief lease of life, but for all time. He built his tower to stand for ages, and it has done so. It is a very perfect specimen of these curious structures that abound in Ireland. It is ninety-five feet high and fifty-three feet in circumference. It is divided into three storeys with loopholes for light and air. The door is twelve feet from the ground. The tower tapers at the top like a sugar loaf, and it was formerly covered with a granite cap, but in the year 1822 it was struck by lightning and was re-roofed. It stands—a strange monument of ancient history—in the centre of well kept grassy lawns, and the secret of why it is there remains a secret still. In the garden beside the tower there is a most curious mass of basalt with two cavities nineteen inches long, sixteen wide, and nine deep. Even in the driest season, they are filled with clear water.

The Parish Church was built in 1595, a small building with Gothic windows. There is a curious tombstone beside the Church which tells us that the colours of a once famous regiment lie buried there. They were cremated and interred in the year 1801. These are the exact words on the tombstone: on one side is "Sacred to the memory of Major James Gibson, D.b. Regt., who died the 28th of August, 1800, aged forty years," and on the other, "Here are interred the ashes of the late colours of the Dumbartonshire Regiment of Fencible Infantry, April 27th, 1801."

Millrow Presbyterian Church is one of the oldest in Ireland. It dates from 1619 and another near it from 1645.

Antrim Castle has a stately entrance and the Tudor gate flanked with two towers is unique. The Castle was built in 1662 by Sir John Clotworthy. He was rewarded by Charles II. with a peerage for services to himself. Antrim Castle is a great mansion set in the midst of lovely surroundings, but it is not endowed with the romance of its nearest neighbour, Shane's Castle. The Speaker's Chair and Mace that were used in the Irish Parliament in Dublin are carefully preserved in the Castle. Massereene means a "beautiful portion" and so it is indeed.

Antrim was for hundreds of years the scene of many conflicts and the town was burned and sacked over and over again. It was plundered and left desolate many times. In one of these terrible struggles it is said 3,000 people were killed. Antrim was one of the centres of the rising in 1798. There was a battle fought and a great many lives lost. The opposing forces met in the streets, and the inhabitants turned out in defence of their homes. Many women and children took refuge under the branches of the trees which overhung the river, and remained there in safety through the long hours of that dreadful day. Lord O'Neill was shot and died on the steps of the Market House. The marks of the bullets are still seen in the spire of the church, for it was in the street beside it the hottest fight took place. So many bullets were embedded in the oak door, that it was afterwards removed, and is still preserved in Antrim Castle. Henry Joy McCracken was the commander of the insurgents in Antrim. He was taken prisoner a few days after the battle, and his life came to an untimely end.

He was universally regretted, but no efforts could avert his sentence. He was hanged at the Market House in High Street in Belfast, and was buried in Belfast, in the graveyard of St. George's Church. He had a fine character, and his unhappy death was deeply deplored by all who knew him.

At one time, there were forty-eight religious establishments in County Antrim alone, and an immense number of ancient fortresses and raths. Interesting remains are still to be seen of the old castles at Greencastle, Olderfleet, Castle Chichester, Red Bay, Castle of Court Martin, Glenville, Dunluce, Dunseverick, Kenbane, Doonaninny, Castle Cary, Bruce's Castle, Castle Upton, Lissanoure, Castle Robin and Portmore. It is impossible to even name them all, but we cannot conclude without mentioning the ruins beside the old Church at Kilroot, where Dean Swift was incumbent for two years[2]. The graveyard is in a disgraceful condition, and the baptismal font is lying in the long grass, totally uncared-for. The rectory where he lived in the year 1695 is beside Kilroot station and is still inhabited.

CHAPTER XXV

SHANE'S CASTLE

Ireland is full of ruined abbeys, monasteries, churches and castles, and almost every small town can tell a tale of departed glory. Howth has a history of its own that is unequalled. Malahide Castle has been for eight hundred years inhabited by successive generations of the same family, and the neighbourhood of Dublin overflows with ancient landmarks.

But we must not wander so far from home, for we have as a near neighbour one of the oldest and most beautiful of them all. Shane's Castle,—or, as it was once called, "Eden-duff-carrick"— has been, since the year 1345, the home of the O'Neills. The Royal house of O'Neill traces its history back to the very beginning of Ireland's story. They were kings of Ulster for one thousand years. Like the branches of a great oak tree that has its roots twined about the very heart of the earth itself, it would be impossible to record a tithe of the events connected with such a people as the O'Neills. From Donegal to Belfast, all Ulster belonged to them, and they were a terror in Ulster until Queen Elizabeth's time.

A clan that could muster 24,500 fighting men was not likely to be easily subdued, and formed a power to be reckoned with. Every schoolboy knows the story of Shane O'Neill's visit to Queen Elizabeth.

Their ancient stronghold was at Dungannon, their kings were

126

elected in the Primate's Palace in Armagh, and inaugurated with crown and golden shoe on the hill at Tullahogue, until the year 1595.

In an ancient expedition for the conquest of Ireland, the leader of it declared that whoever of his followers first touched the shore should possess the territory. One of them, the founder of the race which supplied Ulster with kings for centuries, coveting the reward and seeing that another boat was likely to reach the land before him, seized an axe and with it cut off his left hand, which he flung on shore, and so was the first to touch it. Hence a red hand became the armorial ensign of the province.

But it is their connection with Shane's Castle we have to do with now. In the year 1230, two sons divided into two separate branches, and the younger settled at Lough Neagh, and this castle was first called Eden-duff-carrick when he built it in 1345. Shane MacBrien O'Neill changed the name to Shane's Castle in the year 1722. He was buried in the small graveyard adjoining, and his vault is still preserved. There is an underground passage from the Castle into the graveyard, and another leading to the edge of the water. These underground passages are of spacious and curious construction. One of them is a great kitchen with a fireplace where immense quantities of food could be prepared. There are stables for horses with an entrance under the terrace, and the water of the Lough came close up to the walls at one time. The most important thing was a spring of good water. There is no doubt that these passages were often used, and were found extremely useful during the rough times of former years. The terrace was built about the year 1800, and twenty pieces of cannon dated 1790 are still there. A large addition to the castle was in course of erection when it was irretrievably destroyed by fire in 1816, which was caused by a rook's nest in the chimney taking fire. The entire buildings were ruined, the fortified esplanade, the cannon and a grand conservatory alone being left.

A great library and some most valuable paintings were lost, and the ruins left show that it must have been a spacious and magnificent building. The present Castle was built on the site of the stable yard. It is a commodious residence, but has no stately dignity or striking beauty to mark its outline.

The demesne extends along the shores of Lough Neagh and covers 2,600 acres of most beautiful scenery. The oak trees are the finest in the north of Ireland, and the gardens are famous for their beauty. There is an old story of one owner who, to pay a fine of £30,000, cut down the timber and paid the debt in oak trees, but they are never missed now, for a hundred years can produce more trees.

Shane O'Neill had a printing-press, an unusual possession in those days, and he had also a chess board formed of the bones of the men of Leinster who were ancient enemies of the race.

Ram's Island on Lough Neagh, six acres in extent, and Bird Island, a smaller place near it, are both very lovely. Ram's Island was once named Inis Island, and a great many years ago it belonged to an old fisherman who obtained possession by prescriptive right. A man called Conway MacNiece bought it from him for one hundred guineas. It then passed into the possession of a man named Whittle, who did much to beautify it. He planted an orchard and made a garden and did a great deal to embellish

Old Long Bridge, Belfast, 1836.

BELFAST HARBOUR.
ABOUT 1875.

BELFAST HARBOUR FROM THE CUSTOM HOUSE.
ON THE DAY OF THE OPENING OF THE NEW CHANNEL, 10ᵀᴴ JULY 1849.

THE HARBOUR OFFICE, CORPORATION SQUARE, BELFAST.

River Scene, Purdysburn, County Down.

LISBURN.

WHERE JEREMY TAYLOR WAS BISHOP.

LONDONDERRY.
(FROM W.H. BARTLETT.)

THE LINEN INDUSTRY.
I.—SOWING THE FLAX SEED.

THE LINEN INDUSTRY.
II.—STEEPING THE FLAX.

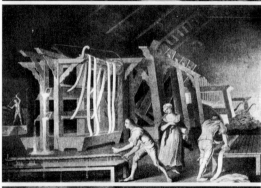

THE LINEN INDUSTRY.
III.—PREPARING THE YARN.

THE LINEN INDUSTRY.
IV.—STAMPING THE LINEN.

BELFAST SHIPYARD, 1812.

LAUNCH OF THE FIRST WOODEN STEAMSHIP *AURORA*, BELFAST. 1824.

DEAN SWIFT'S RECTORY, 1695.
KILROOT.

THE TOWER OF SHANE'S CASTLE.
BUILT 1345; BURNED 1816.

North Gate, Carrickfergus.

CARRICKFERGUS CASTLE.
FROM W.H. BARTLETT'S 'SCENERY AND ANTIQUITIES OF IRELAND'.

OLD CASTLE IN BANGOR, 1600.
FROM A VERY OLD PAINTING.

LARNE.
AFTER W.H. BARTLETT.

its natural loveliness. He planted hundreds of rose trees. Whittle, who lived in Glenavy, got the island in exchange for a farm, and some time afterwards Lord O'Neill bought it from him. Ram's Island has been the property of the O'Neill family since then.

Lord O'Neill then built a cottage on the island for occasional residence. The ruins of a round tower and remnant of an old church are still to be seen on the island. Many traditions linger on the shores of Lough Neagh, and the water is said to petrify wood, but a more miraculous quality is ascribed to it. On Midsummer Eve great crowds used to come to bathe in the water to cure all sorts of sickness, and herds of cattle were driven into it for the same purpose.

Such a place as Shane's Castle is full of romance, and when we gaze at the ivy-clad walls of the magnificent ruins, or listen to the music of the river as it hastens to the Lough, we can readily believe that the O'Neill Banshee still appears wandering in the moonlight under the shade of the ancient trees.

Many of the old families in Ireland are believed to have one of these spirits attending them, but in none is there more faith than in the O'Neill's Banshee. She comes to forewarn death by melancholy wailings. "Maoveen"—little Mab—is her name. Vallancey[1] calls her the "angel of death" or separation. Lady Morgan, more poetically, names her "the white lady of sorrow." To doubt the existence of "Maoveen" is never thought of, and indeed all the surroundings favour the idea.

There is a head carved in stone on one of the walls of the ruined Castle, and tradition says that, when it falls, the race will be extinct. It is already loose and tottering, but the race lives on and the head still holds its position. There are few places that live in remembrance like Shane's Castle, few places where superstition is so easily stirred. If we wander under the shadow of the spreading trees, or linger near the little graveyard with its gloomy vault, or stand beside the crumbling walls of the stately towers, we are awed by the thought of all that has come and gone in O'Neill's history since the day the bloody hand first touched the shore. It matters not if we see it in all the green glory of summer sunshine, or in the pale misty moonlight of a still evening, there is no place that can be compared to it. There is, and can be, but one Shane's Castle—it stands alone in a beauty all its own.

CHAPTER XXVI

CARRICKFERGUS

Carrickfergus is about eight miles distant from Belfast. Carrickfergus! The very name carries us away back into the twilight of Irish history. It was once the central point of warfare, standing in the forefront of many a desperate conflict, and it is full of history and romance. Truth and fiction are so interwoven in any place of such antiquity that the task of sifting the facts is not an easy one. We know enough, however, from reliable sources to form a fair idea of the story of one of the oldest towns in Ireland, and many ancient remains of former greatness are still seen which confirm the tale.

Looking at the quiet old town to-day one can scarcely believe that it was once a place of the greatest importance, and the centre of such stirring times, when Belfast was only a small village. The oldest records tell us that an Irish King, Feargus, built the first castle to defend his property three hundred and twenty years before Christ. He crossed to Scotland, and on his return journey he was wrecked on a rock in the bay, called afterwards the Rock of Fergus. His body was found and buried in the adjacent abbey of Monkstown. Another story tells that the same rock was called Carraig-na-Fairge, rock of the sea, from which it is more probable the name Carrickfergus was derived. From that time until a hundred years ago, Carrickfergus suffered almost constant invasion, plunder, bloodshed and burning.

The Castle, the Church and remains of the walls bear silent witness to the oft-told story. The first wall was built round the city inside a month. It was built of sods and the inhabitants all joined with alacrity to defend the place from their enemies. This wall was afterwards replaced by stone, part of which is still to be seen. It was eighteen feet high, six feet thick and had seven bastions. The corners were of cut yellow stone, freestone, not found in any place in the neighbourhood. A moat safeguarded the landward side, a deep trench and drawbridge the outer side. There were four gates—The Glenarm or Spittal Gate—now the North Gate, the Woodburn or West Gate, the Water Gate and the Finey Gate which had battlements on the top. James I. entered the town by a drawbridge.

The North Gate is still a picturesque memorial of the old days, but we hope the ancient structure may not fulfil the tradition which says: "The North Gate will stand until a wise man becomes a member of the Corporation." A recent resolution was passed which proves that wise men have now a majority on the Corporation, for they have decided to restore the North Gate. Long may it remain as a most interesting object.

It was in the thirteenth century that Carrickfergus was a walled city. It had a Mayor and Guild borough. The country then was alive with game, hare, wild deer and wolf. There was a grand hunting hill above the city.

In October, 1574, the Mayor and the Corporation took very strong measures to put down scolding. Such "skolds"[1] were to be drawn at "sterne of boate from Peare round the Castell," and afterwards exposed in a cage which stood on the quay. History does not relate how many "skolds" survived this drastic treatment long enough to also stand in a cage. History also carefully avoids stating whether this law was equally enforced for men and women, but we may suppose the law was impartial. The scolding stone was still on the quay until a few years ago.

Some of the old laws were very severe, and we find, in the year 1614, before the judges in the Castle, that a man who stole three cows, worth twenty shillings each, was sentenced to be executed, but one, who struck a woman on the head with a "cudgill" so that she died, was only branded on the left arm and delivered to the Ordinary. They must have been poor specimens of men if they were not worth more than three cows or five shillings worth of a bridle. The sinner who used the "cudgill" was lightly punished, but then it was only a woman—not three cows. A man in Belfast stole a piece of iron worth two shillings, a mantle worth six shillings, and a "chizell" worth eightpence, and he was executed. A woman stole a purse with fifty shillings and she was executed, but a man who beat a woman with a stick until she died, was found "not guilty". Even in those ancient times law does not appear to have been always justice, and it was decidedly in need of being improved, especially from a woman's point of view.

The original charter of the Guild of Carrickfergus is still kept in the Town Hall along with the freeman's roll, the records, and the sword and mace.

The most ancient correct plan of Carrickfergus is dated 1550. In the year 1775, a great storm swept over Carrickfergus, which was accompanied with most violent thunder. The country people said it was a battle between the Scotch and Irish fairies, but no one ever knew which side was victorious.

A stately ceremony was kept up until 1739, in which public proclamations were read at each gate, beginning at the castle. Each man who followed the Mayor rode on horseback with his sword drawn. Afterwards the swords were sheathed when they went to a great banquet given by the Mayor.

One very pleasant memory lingers about the ancient city. There was more charity shown to the poor in Carrickfergus than in any other place in Ireland. No hospital was required, and several of the inhabitants left money to build almshouses for the poor, and also large sums for endowment. This is a happy record for any town to possess.

It is round the Castle that ancient history lingers. The present building was erected by De Courci about the year 1178. It is the only existing edifice in the kingdom which exhibits the old Norman military stronghold, and it is justly considered one of the noblest fortresses of that time now left in Ireland.

It stands on a rocky peninsula thirty feet high, washed on three sides by the sea. Viewed from any point, it presents a most picturesque appearance with its massive walls surmounted with cannon, its ancient gateway with flanking towers and portcullis. One tower is still known as the "Lion's Den", with vaults underneath. The ancient custom is still kept up, and the Mayor of the town is sworn into office in the Castle yard.

The keep is ninety feet high with walls nine feet thick. It is ascended by a winding staircase with loopholes for light and air. It is five storeys high and the lower part is used as a magazine. On the third storey, a room is still named "Fergus' Dining-room"; it is forty feet long, thirty-eight wide and twenty-six feet high, and is a noble apartment.

One inestimable boon was a well inside the building with a never-failing supply of good spring water.

Conn O'Neill was imprisoned in the Castle in the year 1606. I think it was of Conn O'Neill the story was told that some friend sent him a large loaf of bread one day, with a strong fine rope concealed inside, and with it he was able to drop over the prison wall. He made his escape, but returned some time after and was again taken prisoner, when all his vast estates were confiscated. Queen Elizabeth made an order that the Governor of Carrickfergus Castle must always be an Englishman. It was a position more renowned for honour than wealth, for the salary was only £40 a year. We must not linger on the Castle, but touch lightly on the Church. St. Nicholas' Church is built upon the site of a Franciscan monastery. Sir Samuel Ferguson tells in thrilling language of how Corby MacGilmore took refuge at the altar of the old monastery and met with a cruel death even in sanctuary. He had sacked forty monasteries, and sent the monks out to beg their bread, homeless and penniless. He brought back the sacred vessels to lay at the altar, but even the tardy restoration did not save him from his pursuers. There is a subterranean passage under the altar which once led to the ancient monastery, and it can still be traced.

There are some very old painted windows and one transept is filled with monuments of the Donegall family, curious kneeling figures, and the old banners hung from the roof until quite recently. There is a figure of Sir Arthur Moyle on his knees, without any hands, as he lost both hands in Spain when fighting against the Moors. Lord Donegall built a fine mansion on the site of another monastery which was suppressed in the year 1610. The gaol and courthouse now stand upon part of the ground which formerly belonged to the noble house of Joymount. Lord Donegall had spacious gardens round his residence at Joymount. The gaol and courthouse figure largely in history. It was a ghastly custom to spike the heads of the enemies over the gateway, and to allow the blackened heads to be exhibited in such cruel fashion. O'Hagan's head was there so long than an eagle picked the eyes out, and a wren built its nest inside the empty skull, a strange home in which to bring up its family. In the year 1408, there were forty ecclesiastical edifices round about Carrickfergus. A famous priory at Woodburn was called "The Palace" in the year 1326. Long before then, a nunnery had been established at Glynn by Darerca, St. Patrick's sister. There were a great many others, which have been altogether lost sight of. There was a hospital for lepers called St. Bridget's outside the Spittal Gate, and another called Bridewell. The lands adjoining are still called the Spittal Parks. Rumour states that St. Patrick blessed a well and endowed it with miraculous powers of healing. Rumour makes many statements about our patron saint, but in any case St. Patrick's well still exists.

Romance tells us many tales about the unfortunate Edward Bruce who was king for such a brief period, and who was in Carrickfergus in the year 1315. King Robert Bruce of Bannockburn besieged the city of Carrickfergus for twelve months, and he lived there for some time. Then the two brothers left with an army of twenty thousand men, but utter devastation followed, and their later history vibrates with romance and eventful incidents. The end was a sorrowful one. Robert returned to Scotland, Edward was killed in a battle near Dundalk, his head, along with Brian O'Neill's, was salted, and both were sent to King Edward II. at London. A ghastly present for royalty to receive!

The town has a Scotch quarter where the Scotch fishermen lived. A curious custom prevailed among them, that married women never took their husband's name, but retained their own maiden name. The Irish quarter was once called the west suburb. An old signboard used to hang out over a doorway inscribed with this quaint legend,

My ale is good, my measure just
I keep no clerk, and give no trust.

Surely a good sound principle to do business on.

Cairns, raths and ancient remains abound all round Carrickfergus, which will well repay a visit. A curious relic of the old times remained until the nineteenth century. The "Three Sisters" formed a landmark on the low-lying ground bordering the seashore, and the wooden gibbets where malefactors were hanged, were ghastly objects. The last time they were used, three men were hanged. Seven were sometimes hung at one time, and the tall black crosses stood as a silent warning to evil-doers. It was a place to hasten past in the falling dusk, and no one ever cared to linger on that desolate dreary stretch of shore. Though the gruesome crosses have disappeared long since, the place is still an uninviting waste of marshy ground.

CHAPTER XXVII

HOLYWOOD

We know Holywood now as a pleasant place of residence a very short distance from the busy streets of Belfast. Ardmacnissa or "Sanctus Boscus" was once known as a large religious settlement. An ancient church was presided over by St. Laisren in 642, and the only means now of tracing the site is by the "Mound" which still remains in the grounds of Riverston. The ruins of the church were in the vicinity of the funeral mound called Ard-mac-nasca, and the Holy Wood stood on the hill above.

We next find mention of a Franciscan Monastery which was built on the same site in the year 1200. Ten years later King John passed through the little town, and a roll is still preserved in the Tower of London which tells us that he spent a day in "Haliwode".

Brian O'Neill came down upon Holywood in the year 1572, and he burned the church and destroyed all he could lay his hands on.

The town passed into Sir James Hamilton's possession in the year 1606, and a few years later he built another church, and used part of the ruins of the old one. It is a curious structure and some thirteenth-century windows are still to be seen. The tower and walls are a great age, and the small windows above belong to the fifteenth century. It was used for service until the erection of the present church. The holy water stoup was a basin of pure white marble. It was found in the graveyard, and is now used in the new church. The graveyard extended over the Crescent and on to the Mound. A convent once stood near Holywood House which was built in the year 1605. The road leading up to the wood is still called the "Nun's Walk". In the garden of Holywood House, fragments of tombstones and part of a cross have been found. The name survives in the Priory House and Priory Park.

The Roman Catholic Chapel was built in 1872, and the foundation stone was brought from the ruined church of Cartan in Donegal where St. Colombkille[1] was born.

A very good description of the pleasant little town is given in a poem written in the year 1822, which holds good to the present day.

> Close by the water's farther side,
> There sits in clean and modest pride,
> The cheerful little Holywood.

CHAPTER XXVIII

BANGOR

The town of Bangor is situated on the County Down side of the entrance to Belfast Lough. It is about ten miles distant from Belfast, and is a very popular and prosperous seaside town and a favourite holiday resort. It resembles Armagh and Carrickfergus in being full of ancient history, and, like them, it has also passed through many vicissitudes, but all the dark and troubled times are now almost forgotten. The Bangor we know to-day is a more prosperous place than it ever was before. The change and improvement within the last ten years is remarkable, and every year seems to extend the town.

Centuries before Belfast was ever heard of, the town of Bangor was known all over Europe for the great College and the beautiful Abbey Church. In the ancient history of Ireland, Bangor held a very important place. In the year 555 A.D., St. Comgall built an Abbey for Regular Canons, which was the foundation of a town later on. He presided over it for fifty years, and when he died his body was enshrined in it. Some time after the great School of Learning was established, and in process of time it became one of the most eminent colleges in Europe. Many persons of distinction and of the highest rank sent their young men to be educated in Bangor College.

When King Alfred the Great wanted professors for Oxford,

he sent to the great school at Bangor for the teachers he required. As Sir James Ware, the well-known authority, truly says, "The English Saxons received their education from Irish schools." Bangor was the quiet and peaceful habitation of sanctity and learning. A colony of students which varied in numbers from two to four thousand left an indelible mark upon the history of the land. There were men renowned for their power and wisdom, leaders of the people by their counsels and knowledge. They were honoured in their generations, and were the glory of their time. A strange confirmation of the numbers attending the College was recently discovered in the Library in Oxford when an ancient manuscript roll was found containing the names of three thousand students in Bangor.

The original Psalter written by St. Comgall in the Abbey, the "Antiphonary of Bangor", a curious ancient "Book of Anthems" in Latin, was carried by an Irish monk to Bobbio, and is now one of the most precious volumes in the Library of Milan. The Abbey and College prospered for many years until the Danes invaded Bangor in the year 822 A.D., and, as no man is lord of his own any longer than he can defend it against others, so the monks were overcome, and the invaders ruthlessly massacred the Abbot and nine hundred monks. They desecrated the shrine of St. Comgall and left a trail of desolation behind them. The Abbey was rebuilt by St. Malachy, who planned it after the Model of Armagh, at that time (1125) the largest church in Ireland. It was the custom which the Irish tenaciously adhered to, to build them exactly the size St. Patrick had made so many throughout the country, sixty feet long and twenty-five wide. The new church was a magnificent building one hundred and forty feet long, it was called "Pulchro Choro"—"the fair white Choir", from the beautiful white stone and lime that was used for the first time in Ulster. Traces of the old foundations are still visible. Bangor was known at that time as the "Vale of Angels".

The town suffered many times from invasion and still the Abbey lived on. The Church of Bangor was built within the precincts of the Abbey in the year 1617, and it was finished in the year 1623; both dates are cut on a stone set into the south wall, and are also carved on an old oak pulpit. A legend still lingers that there was a secret passage from the old Abbey out to the sea, opening at a point called "Jeannie Watt's Cave"[1]. Adventurous boys have often tried to go through, but a short length of the cave generally proves quite long enough. We can well believe such passages were a dire necessity in times of trouble. The old church was found unsuitable in many ways, and some years ago a very handsome new building was erected on a central site in the town. The old bell of Bangor is now in the possession of Colonel McCance of Knocknagoney.

The castle was built in the year 1600, on the site of an older castle. The Market House has a story connected with it too, for it was there the women and children were placed for protection during the terrible scenes of 1798. The guns and pikes were kept for many years behind the church doors in readiness for any sudden emergency—a vivid memory of stirring times. One very pleasant remembrance of Bangor is the fact that the first Sunday School ever formed in Ireland was at Rath-Gael. It was established by R. J. Cleland, Esq., in the year 1788.

In the year 1831, Mr. James Cleland of Rath-Gael brought six snakes to Ireland. There was great indignation when it became known that he had turned them out into the fields, but four were killed and two lost.

There are the remains of twenty-five forts and raths in the parish, but the largest is at Rath-Gael. It covers two acres, and is surrounded by a double vallum. The first body of English forces under the Duke of Schomberg anchored in Groomsport Bay with 10,000 men, a small fishing village near Bangor which was formerly called "Graham's Port". King William afterwards created the Duke "Earl of Bangor", but he will always be known as Schomberg. It seems difficult to believe the Bangor of the olden time that suffered such severe disaster through plunder, fire and invasion can be the pleasant smiling place we are now familiar with.

Almost every general shop shows festoons of sand shoes, cascades of little buckets and bunches of wooden spades to delight the heart of the young Belfastians. The small builders design some wondrous architecture on the sandy beach, while the older generation disport themselves in the blue waters of the bay.

Long may Bangor flourish as a health-giving outlet for the city of Belfast.

CHAPTER XXIX

GREYABBEY

Greyabbey lies on the shores of Strangford Lough, about fifteen miles from Belfast, and it has a very romantic story to tell. It was built as a thank-offering to God for merciful deliverance from the dangers of the sea.

The famous De Courci married Affrica the daughter of Godred, King of Man. When she was crossing the sea at one time to return home, a great storm arose and the vessel was in imminent danger of being wrecked. Affrica vowed that, if she arrived safely in Ireland, she would build a house in honour of the Virgin.

An angel appeared to her and she had a miraculous passage home—we may suppose under the guidance of the angel. She built Greyabbey in the year 1193, and she brought some monks over from the Cistercian Abbey of Holm Cultram in Cumberland.

As was usually the case, it was built in a secluded sheltered spot, well-wooded hills beside it and a clear stream of water and never-failing springs. The ruined remains are most beautiful and picturesque, and the building must once have been of great extent.

The eastern gable is nearly entire; it has seven windows, and the stone work is almost perfect. The north and south walls have each similar lancet-shaped windows. The nave was used as the parish church until 1778, and is still in good condition. Remains of several very ancient monuments are still existing, and within the choir are two recumbent effigies, carved in freestone, of John De Courci and Affrica his wife. The sculptured decorations of the chapter house show that it must once have been singularly beautiful.

The walls trace the extent of the rooms, and the plan of the building can be clearly defined. There must have been a large colony of monks living at Greyabbey. The refectory, the buttery and the kitchen, with the passages and the remains of a stone staircase are still seen, while the outside buildings cover a considerable area.

When the dissolution of monasteries took place in the year 1536, Greyabbey lived on for thirty years longer, but at the end of Elizabeth's reign it was almost destroyed, and later on Cromwell's men ruined the remainder. What is left now shows that Greyabbey must once have been a stately pile of buildings of more than usual beauty, and even yet it breathes an atmosphere of monastic peace and calm repose.

The foundation walls of an older building have been found in a neighbouring village. A very large tumulus was opened in the year 1825, and a most remarkable discovery was made. Seventeen stone coffins were found, formed by placing together several flagstones on edge, and covering with one large stone. The cavity in the centre was larger than the others, and in each was found an urn of baked clay, containing dark coloured earth. How we would like to know the story that lies buried there!

Greyabbey is the property of the Montgomery family, who have resided in the mansion house of Rosemount since 1622.

The house was burned three times, and this present house is the third built on the same site on the east side of Strangford Lough. Rosemount was built in 1762. The Montgomerys came to Ireland about four hundred years ago. On the summit of a hill near, there is a beautiful little building, a model of the Temple of the Winds at Athens, and the view from the doorway well repays the ascent of the hill.

The remains of Blackabbey are also full of interest. It was part of a great Benedictine monastery built also by De Courci, and there is an underground passage from Greyabbey, which is one mile distant. Blackabbey fell into O'Neill's hands and was finally granted to the Archbishop of Armagh.

At Cloughy there are the ruins of another abbey of the Knights of St. John; also the remains of Slane Church and Kirkstown Castle.

The demesne of Mount Stewart is in the same neighbourhood. The residence of Lord Londonderry, it stands on the shores of Strangford Lough, and is built from stone quarried from Scrabo Hill. The monument which crowns Scrabo is a striking feature in the country. It was built in memory of a former Marquis of Londonderry, and commands a really magnificent prospect. An old ballad written and sung a great many years ago says,

> Oh, Scrabo Hill, that mountain bonnie,
> That hides my love from me;
> I'll bore a hole through Scrabo's side
> And then my love I'll see.

The hole has never been bored through yet, but who knows!

some day it may be. There are a great many places of interest round the shores of Strangford Lough. The name indicates the meaning of "Strong Ford" and woe betide the unwary traveller who faces the force of that inland sea when the tide turns!

Its surface is dotted with three hundred small islands some of which are well worth a visit. The town of Newtownards lies a few miles from Mount Stewart and has a handsome old church and several points of interest. One house still bears this humble inscription on the front.

Not by my merit do I inherit.

Meritorious or not, he did not object to accept the inheritance.

A very long time ago, some Dutchmen offered to buy out a large tract of land at Newtownards, as they found it was extremely suitable for growing herbs, and they wished to develop their cultivation. However, the town refused their offer and the medical profession lost the herbs. The same ground now produces some of the most beautiful roses in the world, so we have fragrance and beauty instead of medicinal herbs.

The little town of Comber lies adjacent to Newtownards, and an Abbey for Cistercian Monks was founded there by De Courci in the year 1199, and again St. Patrick is said to have been the founder of an Abbey of Regular Canons. Comber is better known now as the early home of a very famous man. A stranger passing through the central square of the quiet little town is immediately arrested by a tall column, which forms a striking feature in the place. It is a monument to the memory of Comber's great warrior, Sir Robert Rollo Gillespie, who was born in Comber in the year 1766. He entered the army at an early age and had a long and glorious career. Once, when living at Port-au-Prince, his house was attacked by assassins. Armed only with his sword, he courageously attacked them. He killed six and the rest fled in terror. He was in many conflicts, was at the taking of Vellore, Cornells, and Java. He was commander of the famous expedition in 1811 to Meerut. Leading his men in a desperate attack on Kalanga, he was shot near the walls. With the red stream of his life blood flowing, he raised his voice in a last shout and cried, "One shot more for the honour of Down."

A memorial was raised over his grave at Meerut, and a statue erected in St. Paul's Cathedral to honour his name, but perhaps the monument raised by his townsmen speaks most eloquently of his worth, and the affectionate remembrance of those who knew him best.

CHAPTER XXX

ARDGLASS

Ardglass takes its name from "Ardholl" the High Green from the lofty ward hill. It was in former days a place of great importance, a corporate town and a royal borough sending members to Parliament. It was once the second town in Ulster, and was next to Carrickfergus as a seat of trade, being one of the most important seaports, and it was also a place of immense military strength. No other town in the country ever was so well fortified. It has a most imposing situation and an extensive view of the Irish Sea, the Isle of Man, and the blue hills of Galloway along the horizon.

The great number of fortified and castellated edifices gives the place a unique appearance, which renders its present obscurity all the more remarkable.

Ancient records tell us that a monastery was there which was founded—as usual—by St. Patrick, but it is not like the kind of place where a monastery would probably be built. Safer and more sheltered situations were more frequently used.

There was a large parish church on the top of a hill where a terrible disaster once occurred. On a Christmas night when there was a large congregation assembled, a hostile clan descended upon them, and there was a dreadful scene of murder. After this outbreak the church was abandoned and another built lower down. Ardglass is now chiefly remarkable for the number of very old castles, nearly all in ruins, but all pointing to the broken glory of departed days. Only the shell of some remain, but even those old walls are vibrant with romance. Some of them are said to have been built by De Courci and most likely were, as they date from the twelfth century. The largest is King's Castle, a fortress of great size.

Jordan's Castle was besieged for three years in the time of Queen Elizabeth. It was a finer building than any of the others, and a place of considerable strength. The armorial bearings of the family are cut in the stone, a cross and three horseshoes. There is Margaret's Castle and Tower and Horn Castle, so named from the possession of some curious horns found near Ardglass Castle. A strange name is Coud Castle[1], which means "without horns". Another stands detached beside a most remarkable pile of buildings which were erected by Shane O'Neill in the year 1570. It is a long range of castellated houses extending for 234 feet. A battlement surmounts the inward side, and a wide platform is built along the front, and there are three towers at equal distance, fifteen arched doorways of cut stone, and sixteen square windows. They may have once been used for shops. The upper storey is exactly the same, and each has a separate stone staircase, but there is no fireplace in all the building. This strange line of old houses tells its silent tale of the past. It is rather sad to see a place so full of ruins, and with so much buried history that we shall in all probability never now find out.

After the rebellion of 1641, Ardglass rapidly declined, until now it is a veritable sleepy hollow, and its fishing industry is almost all that is left of its former greatness.

The railway may—let us hope—prove a benefit to the town[2], and also the golf links. Ardglass has all the natural advantages that go to make a prosperous watering-place. It has most lovely surroundings, fine air, and a wide open sea front with a stretch of view unsurpassed. It only requires to be better known, for, to a great many people, Ardglass is only a name.

CHAPTER XXXI

DOWNPATRICK

Downpatrick is only eighteen miles from Belfast, but it seems to belong to the "land of long ago". The story of St. Patrick is closely entwined with Downpatrick, and the country surrounding it. Here he founded one of the earliest abbeys in Ireland in the year 493 A.D., the Abbey for Canons Regular, but it met with the usual fate and was destroyed, was rebuilt and destroyed again. The town is built on a group of little hills. Ptolemy mentioned it as Dunum, and few towns can boast of a more ancient foundation. Downpatrick figures prominently in monastic story and popular legend. It was burnt six or seven times and the cathedral was pillaged every time. Several Priory churches were erected. When De Courci rebuilt the cathedral in 1185, he found the remains of the original figures of St. Patrick, St. Bridget and St. Columba, and he placed them on shrines inside the Abbey. But the statues met with a sad fate in the year 1538. Lord Leonard de Grey wilfully defaced them, and he too met with a sad fate, for he was beheaded for this act of desecration.

The venerable and beautiful structure was taken down in 1790 to allow a new building to be erected on the same site. It was completed in 1829, and the mutilated figures were placed over the east window. A round tower sixty-six feet high formerly stood at the western end of the cathedral, but unfortunately it had to be taken down, as its ruinous condition threatened to injure the church. A fine old Celtic cross was also removed from the street, and it is now behind the chapel. Dun-Padriug[1]—the hill of Patrick—was once known as Rath-Celtchair, and it is the largest hill fort in the province. It is a short distance from the north side of the cathedral and is a very ancient structure. It measures 895 yards at the base, and is surrounded by three ramparts. In the year 1259, there was a great battle fought in the streets between Lord Justice Stephen De Long Epée, and the Irish chieftain O'Neill. O'Neill and 352 men were killed. In 1246, part of the abbey was destroyed by an earthquake; Edward Bruce plundered and wasted it still more, and burnt the town. Three years later, he returned and again plundered the abbey, and he proclaimed himself King of Ireland at the cross near the cathedral.

Downpatrick was the chosen place of residence of many of the Kings of Ulster, and in addition to the abbey founded by St. Patrick, we read of four priories, one of which and a leper hospital were founded by De Courci. The story of the life and death of De Courci is closely interwoven with the history of Downpatrick, where he lived in regal state and where he was finally taken prisoner. He was a man of immense size and strength and of great courage. He once challenged Sir Hugh De Lacy to fight him in single combat but De Lacy refused, saying it was not fit for the King's representative to fight with a rebel. He bribed some servants to attack De Courci when he was kneeling at prayer in the graveyard. He was unarmed and was only clad in linen garments, but he seized a large wooden cross and killed thirteen of his opponents, and he was finally overcome and taken prisoner. The end of his life is of thrilling interest and well repays perusal. The ruins of the cathedral stood for two hundred and fifty years, and part of it was used in the rebuilding. The famous Jeremy Taylor was Bishop for some time. The Gaol, Hospitals and County Court House are all handsome buildings.

The Abbey of Saul

Saul Abbey is one mile from Downpatrick, the Latin name is "Saballum"; in Irish it is "Sgibot-Phadraig" Patrick's Barn. The cry of Patrick was "Come and be saved" which was corrupted into "Samall" to save, still further changed into "Saul". There is another story of how this curious name originated. An Irish chieftain named Dichu gave St. Patrick a barn to be used as a church, and gave him also a piece of ground to be used as a site for building a church upon, so "Patrick's Barn" arose. This was the first monastery in Ireland and was built by St. Patrick in the year 432 A.D.; the old church was of cruciform shape and covered a considerable extent of ground. St. Patrick died in Saul at the great age of one hundred and twenty years. He dearly loved the quiet peaceful spot, and his grave is near the door of the Cathedral in Downpatrick, but the memory of his long and useful life will be for ever fragrant in Ireland. It will always be as fresh as the shamrock and as green as an emerald.

The greater part of the church has now disappeared, but a small cell with a curiously high-pitched roof is still in the churchyard. It is said to be the tomb of Malachi O'Morgair, a once famous Bishop of Down. There is a fine slab, with an incised cross on it, set into the gate wall. Some rude stone crosses lie among the grass and numerous stone coffins, and the graveyard is crowded to excess. The ruins of an embattled castle and two small towers stand near the old church. A mile south of the hill of Slieve-na-Griddle are the wells of Struel, four holy wells each covered with a vault of stone. On Midsummer Eve, great crowds of people used to assemble, some for penance, and some seeking for health.

The Eye Well is in the centre of a green space, and exactly at twelve o'clock the water of the well overflows and fills the green; it remains for half an hour and then subsides until the next Midsummer Eve. The people believe in the water having a miraculous healing power for spiritual as well as bodily disease. There are four wells, the Body and the Well of Sins, the Limb Well, the Eye Well, and the Well of Life. It has been discovered that the wells are all connected by a subterranean stream. The name Struel comes from an Irish word "struthair", a stream. Near the old Chapel on the brow of a hill is a stone chair known as St. Patrick's Chair. There is also a remarkable Druidical altar, and, in the same neighbourhood in the year 1834, a beautiful gold torque was found which was richly ornamented and set with gems, truly a relic of olden times.

CHAPTER XXXII

NEWRY

We find Newry is mentioned in ancient MSS., 900 years before Christ. It is in the richest part of Ulster, a post, market, and seaport town of most ancient history. It lies thirty miles southwest of Belfast. The massive form of Slieve-gullion and the romantic outlines of the Mourne Mountains with the addition of the surpassing beauty of Carlingford Lough would make Newry a place full of interest, but when we know that, from the earliest ages, it was renowned for its sacred buildings and famous School of Learning, we find Newry is one of the most important of our old towns.

A desperate battle took place in the year 332 A.D. A rampart was built from Scarva extending to Jonesborough, still called the "Dane's Cast" which was a marvellous piece of work to have been done fifteen hundred years ago. St. Patrick gave the name "Na Yur", the yew tree at the head of the strand. He planted the yew trees and one great tree which overshadowed the abbey gate. A Cistercian abbey was founded in the year 1153, by King Morice McLoghlin[1], who got the consent of all the kings and peers in Ulster and Errigal to open it, and is almost the only monastic charter in existence. It is a most curious and unique document, and it is now kept in the British Museum.

A celebrated grove of yew trees was afterwards on the site

of the abbey and two remarkable trees were called the Newries. Several of the yew trees still flourish, and are still evergreen.

One of the most famous of the collegiate schools was in Newry and it was there King Alfred the Great was sent to receive his education.

Newry was granted to Sir Richard Bagnal, and he turned the beautiful territory of the abbey grounds into his own palace garden. He built St. Patrick's Church in 1578, and it was destroyed in 1641, but after the restoration it was repaired, re-roofed and enlarged. A castle built by De Courci was destroyed by Edward Bruce, and it was rebuilt and again destroyed by Shane O'Neill. But the most disastrous destruction was done by James II. who left only one castle and six houses. All the houses in Newry were formerly built of granite, but ruthless and utterly useless devastation seemed the usual line of treatment in those old times. There are in Newry two St. Patrick's and two St. Mary's. The Roman Catholic St. Patrick's is a very handsome Gothic structure and a place of considerable monastic celebrity. Human remains of a very large size were dug up near the abbey. They had shoes on the feet. Bishops and abbots were formerly buried with shoes on their feet.

The men of the Kingdom of Mourne were said to be the finest-looking men to be found in all Ireland, and old writers say that Newry claims the honour of having the most beautiful women in Ireland, and that no other part of the country can show so much character to correspond.

The greatest cattle drive in all history occurred in Mourne when Turlough O'Neill carried off at Kilmorey 3,000 cows belonging to Sir Richard Bagnal and the Dean of Armagh, in the year 1557.

In the year 1814, during some excavations, a large quantity of coins were found near Newry. Two hundred were found at Castle Lenahan which were enclosed in a cow's horn, and had been buried in the earth. Some bore the head of Edward I., and some the head of Robert Bruce, and they had been buried for 500 years. In a bog at a place called Lougriecouse, there was found, twenty-three feet below the surface, the body of a Highlander fully dressed. The dress was perfect but the body crumbled away when it was moved. Newry is now a pleasant thriving business town, and the memory of the old times still lingers.

CHAPTER XXXIII

CARLINGFORD

The history of Carlingford goes back to the time when St. Patrick returned to Ireland, for it was here that he landed. The first time, it is said, he landed at Dundrum.

It was once a fortified town, and part of the wall still remaining shows that it was of great thickness and strength. There were thirty-two castles and monasteries about Carlingford, so it is rich in castellated and monastic legacies of a proud past.

De Courci seems to have closely followed where St. Patrick marked the way, and he built the castle in 1210. It is named King John's Castle, and is the gem of Carlingford. It is curiously made in the shape of a horse-shoe, owing to the formation of the rock it is built on, and it is a massive pile with walls eleven feet thick. It stands in lonely grandeur, "Moored on a rifted rock"; it once guarded the frontier of Ulster at this narrow pass. It needed no moat, drawbridge or portcullis to repel invaders, for nature supplied all the defence which was required to protect the entrance of Carlingford Lough. The majestic fortress was surrounded by galleries and arched recesses, and each loophole was large enough to hold four or five archers. The dungeons under the castle were hewn out of the solid rock.

The early settlers of the "Pale" flocked to Carlingford for

refuge and protection, and in time it became a place of considerable importance.

In the year 1305, the abbey, a Dominican monastery, was built. The ivy-clad walls show that it was very extensive, and what still remains is extremely picturesque.

To have been erected at such an early period, the architecture is very beautiful and the long aisles, the belfry, and the Gothic arch of the east window are chaste and impressive.

One Lord Inchiquin, in utter disregard for the sacred edifice, turned it into a stable, and this was strangely confirmed some years ago, when some horse-shoes were found imbedded in the floor. In later years, Duke Schomberg's wounded soldiers were brought into the abbey, and it was used for a hospital.

Between the castle and the monastery, there are two square towers which show remains of very curious carving. One tower has a strange device of serpents, human heads and true-lovers'-knots, and the other has a winding staircase leading to the top, from which there is a magnificent view.

There is an old church, a large and handsome building near the abbey, which was erected on the site of an older edifice. The spacious graveyard is remarkable for its vivid greenness, and also for the ancient oak trees and wide-spreading sycamores. A large bell which belonged to the abbey was used in the church, but a rector, for some unknown reason, sold it in Liverpool, where it is still used. It was of ancient Irish work, with a mellow, sonorous sound.

When Henry IV. sent his son over as the Lord Deputy of Ireland in the year 1408, Lord Thomas of Lancaster used to climb to the highest part of the castle wall and sit there to gaze over the glorious prospect which lay at his feet. The place was called the "King's Seat".

A strange old building which looks now like a watch tower was the "Tholsel" a kind of town hall. It is a small rude edifice arched over the narrow street. Small and insignificant as it seems, it was formerly used by the Sovereign of Carlingford and twelve burgesses, who once gave laws to three counties, Louth, Armagh, and Down. What a show-place Carlingford would be made if it were in some English county, with the blue waters of the Lough spreading for miles through such exquisite scenery, and the long chain of rugged mountains—the Ulster Apennines[1]—the guardian sentinels of our northern land.

CHAPTER XXXIV

ROSTREVOR

Every tourist who has seen the placid restful little town echoes the words so often used: "Beautiful Rostrevor". Every guide-book repeats the same and adds, "the sweetest little village under the sun." Words are but a poor medium to express the loveliness of all the surroundings, the wide waters of the bay with the purple-topped mountains of Carlingford in the distance, and the rugged slopes of the Mourne Mountains on the landward side. The silver waters of the river gleaming through the trees, the beautiful old houses with their grassy lawns, and the trees that have stood for hundreds of years, all go to create a picture that lives long in memory.

I do not know any place where there are so many beautiful old houses grouped together within such a short distance from each other. The "Woodhouse", with an exquisite view from its terrace, the "Lodge", with its spreading trees and its famous aviary and well-known collection of animals brought from all parts of the world. Here the snow-white sacred cow from India calmly grazes side by side with a fiery little black bison, and other strange animals with wide-spreading horns, and all live most contentedly together in the fields on the hill-side, while the Indian and Egyptian water-fowl are happy on the river. Then comes "Fairy Hill", and truly a more appropriate name could not have been found for such a place. The "Old Hall" and the "Ghan" are like a breath of other days. "Bladensburgh" is a beautiful demesne, and across the road stands "Carpenham", which takes its curious name from the three first syllables of *Car*oline *Pen*elope *Ham*ilton, which make the word Carpenham. The trees here are most wonderful. The view at "Arno's Vale" and the "Doctor's Walk" must be seen to be understood, and indeed the road to Warrenpoint is a picture all the way.

We may see Rostrevor in the early spring time, when the first primroses appear, or later on when the March winds have shaken out the golden bells of the daffodils, which bloom in thousands under the old trees, or when the wild cherry trees are laden with their snowy burden and make the hill-side of Slieve Bán a thing of beauty. When the glory of summer days has gone, and autumn touches the face of nature with its crimson and gold, the trees along the river-side vie with each other in tints of russet red and golden brown. Then winter comes, and we think each changing season is lovelier than the last, for the glossy green of the holly trees weighed down with the vivid scarlet of the berries against the sober colour of the firs, seems the loveliest picture of the year. Cold and frost do not linger long in Rostrevor's salubrious climate, for the snow may lie in patches beside the "big stone" of Cloughmore, or touch lightly the emerald colour of the "Fiddler's Green", but snow and winter's cold never live long here. Beautiful Rostrevor! it is well named, always fair and smiling, always a haven of rest and peace, a place to go to when we want time to pick up the ravelled threads of life again, and find a quiet breathing-space out of everyday cares and worries. But,—enough about the harmonious beauty of the place, Rostrevor has a very ancient history, and has borne many names. The oldest name is Carrickavraghad, and it was next called Castle Roe and finally Rostrevor. The massive castle, once the stronghold of Rory McGennis, one of the lords of Iveagh—stood near the centre of the town, but now there is not a solitary vestige of the ancient castle left. In the reign of Queen Elizabeth, the place passed into the hands of Sir Marmaduke Whitchurch, and the story of that old romance is worth telling over again. I shall endeavour to do so and condense it as much as possible.

The chieftain of McGennis and the rightful lord of Iveagh was outlawed from his home, and a price was set upon his head. Sir Marmaduke Whitchurch was made owner of the estate, and lived in the ancestral home of Castle Roe. McGennis loved Sir Marmaduke's fair daughter Eva, but his suit seemed hopeless.

One evening, as he was in a boat on the lough, the old boatman told him that night was falling and spoke of the danger of passing Castle Roe. He knew that if any of Sir Marmaduke's men caught sight of the son of their enemy near the castle, he would soon adorn the highest tree in the forest, and be esteemed the most precious fruit it could bear. But the young chieftain was in a reckless mood, and he landed at the little cove and wandered on to the castle, which was the dearest spot on earth to him, and was filled with recollections of the past. Now it was the home of his beloved Eva. The moon was shining softly through the long rows of stately trees, silence reigned supreme, broken only by the murmurs of the ocean as the waves kissed the pebbly beach. He scaled the rampart of the castle at a remote corner, and every window was dark, but one which looked out upon a lawn. Since he was a little child, he had not entered his father's halls, or passed the boundary wall.

At the open window sat Rose Whitchurch and young Edward Trevor, who was a favourite captain of Queen Elizabeth's, and afterwards Baron of Dungannon. They were to be married the next morning.

Sir Marmaduke sat farther from the window with the light from the torches falling on his grey hair and handsome face, while close beside him sat his youngest and best-beloved daughter, Eva. "To-morrow, Rose," he said, "you leave this place for ever. Wood and mountain, hill and valley, sea and sequestered glen, which you know and love so well, after to-morrow will know you no more!"

"Oh! say not so, father," she cried passionately, "I could not bear the thought of leaving Castle Roe and all its charms for ever. Look out, Trevor, and you too, Eva, where would you find on earth a scene of such exquisite beauty? See, the moon touches the tree tops with her silver light, and tinges the faint outline of the distant Foy, and castellated cliffs of Carlingford. See there on the broad breast of Slieve Bán, where Clochmore sits, a feathery cloud rests like a crown upon her brow. Where can the eye take in at one glance so much? Oh! it is as beautiful as—"

"Yourself," exclaimed the enraptured lover.

"Ay, Rose, as you and Trevor," interposed Sir Marmaduke. "From this night it shall no more be known as Castle Roe, but shall be called Rose Trevor!"

McGennis waited long, but could not get a chance of speech

with Eva. She had been kept a prisoner in her father's castle, when he heard of her secret meetings with the son of his old enemy. The next night, he braved the walls again, and was taken prisoner. He heard Eva entreating her father to spare his life, and he with stern voice swear that the next morning would see him hung from the highest tree. Shut in the dungeon keep, there seemed no hope left, but Eva came in the night and set him free. She fled with him, and there on the rugged brow of Slieve Mór they were joined in holy wedlock by the waiting priest. For two years they lived in perfect happiness as only those who live for each other know, but death had marked the gentle Eva for his own, and now a granite-covered grave marks her resting-place in Kilbroney.

CHAPTER XXXV

KILBRONEY

About one mile distant from Rostrevor lies the ancient graveyard of Kilbroney. These lonely little burial-places are frequently met with in quiet out-of-the-way corners. An atmosphere of rest seems to dwell in the seclusion of "God's Acre", and some of them are full of a holy solemnity. I recall the rugged hill-side of the graveyard at Dunluce where Don Alonzo De Leyva and 260 of his men were buried, when the unfortunate *Gerona*[1] was dashed to pieces at Port-na-Spania[2], the old cemetery at Bonamargy, and the one at Knockladye, where the three Princesses lie buried. These all live in memory—beautiful in their loneliness, but they lie on a desolate bare hill-side. Each has its own story and each has a distinct beauty of its own.

The gem of all I have ever seen is at Kilbroney. It lies on the southern slope of a hill that goes down to the river. Oak trees, pines, and larch grow in great luxuriance, and the sun shines through their foliage with golden light, and the grass is greener at Kilbroney than any other place I ever saw. The old church has been in ruins for centuries and *when* it was built no one can tell, but the ruins are of great antiquity. It is uncertain whether the church was dedicated to St. Bruno or took its name from the wood where the broneys or fairies used to live in the good old times. However, it has been in ruins for so long that an oak tree eighty feet high has grown out of the wall, and another out of the floor. The building is very small, as the oldest churches in Ireland were always small, some majestic yew trees flourish near the ancient walls, and the tower is a mass of ivy. Kilbroney had a famous bell called "Clogh-ban", the "white bell", which was known all over the country. When invasion threatened once in the old turbulent times and danger came very near, the precious bell was carefully hidden and safely kept. The danger passed, and, in later years when the new generation wanted the bell, it could not be found. Those who had hidden it had kept the secret so well that when they died it remained a secret still. It became a proverb in the country and people used to say in sceptical tones, "It will happen when Kilbroney bell rings again."

A great many years passed away, so many that the acorns which dropped into a cleft in the wall, and through the broken roof, had time to grow into trees before the bell rang again. One night a terrific storm raged over Kilbroney, and through the pauses when the wind seemed to wait to gather strength for a more violent blast, there was distinctly heard the full, clear sound of a bell ringing. All through that awful night it rang, and when morning came and the storm was over, it was still heard in tones—now high—now low—but full of music. The frightened people came near. There in the ancient tower was the famous bell. It had never been anywhere else, for the old monks had built it in with stones, and no one had ever thought of looking for it there. As years passed away, the tower was covered with ivy and the clinging tendrils had held the stones together until the storm had swept the ivy away, and, when the stones fell down, the bell was once more free to swing to and fro, as it had done hundreds of years before. It was removed from the roofless ruined building and was placed in the new chapel, where it is used every Sunday morning as the altar bell. About the year 1810, three very old candlesticks were found in the ruins, where they must have lain for some centuries—brass candlesticks connected at the sides and bottom. The one in the centre had an inscription, on one was carved a cross, and on the other a hand. But the most curious part of all was that in each candlestick was a piece of wood, wrapped round with wool which had been oiled. The wood was perfectly sound, was easily ignited and retentive of flame, and they were probably used as a substitute for wax tapers before candles were invented, and had evidently been altar lights. Candles were not invented until 1300[3], so these old candlesticks must have been of very ancient date.

A spacious cave was found, containing broken urns which were filled with calcined human bones and ashes. Cremation is a very old fashion revived.

There was also at one time a chalybeate[4] spring, but it fell into disuse long since. A holy well was under the shade of a majestic ash tree, and it was once a favourite place of pilgrimage, but it too has only the memory of departed days.

Some very curious tombstones are in the graveyard, and one stone figure of a child has a strange history. The last Irish giant[5] lies buried here, and an epitaph is on his headstone. In all the land one could not find a lovelier spot than the old peaceful graveyard of Kilbroney.

CHAPTER XXXVI

NARROWWATER CASTLE

Narrowwater Castle is—as its name signifies—built upon a narrow part of the river which flows into Carlingford Lough. The river is half a mile in width before and after passing the projecting rock on which the castle is built. Hugh de Lacy, in the year 1212, erected the first castle on this enormous rock, as a protection for the ferry across the channel.

Later on, the Duke of Ormonde built the present massive and warlike pile in the troubled times of 1663. It consisted of one square battlemented tower standing upon the rock, which was once entirely isolated as the water flowed completely round it. It was a place of great strength, as we see from its discoloured and ominous walls. Memory invests it with many associations. Years have flowed by like the waters it overshadows, and it stands yet unchanged, a grim and silent guardian commanding the entrance to Newry by land as well as sea. The island rock is now no longer an island, a broad road connects it with the mainland, but the rampart on the seaward side is still beaten by the waves.

A romantic story lingers yet, and recalls a vivid picture of life as it was long ago. An Irishman had brought his young and beautiful wife here from the sunny land of Spain. He became wildly jealous of the great admiration her beauty excited, and he imprisoned her in a turret chamber in Narrowwater Castle.

The story of her cruel treatment became known, and an old lover from Spain followed her in the vain hope of setting her free, and taking her back to her own land. Many a long night she sat on the battlements singing the old songs of happier days. Death came to the gentle lady's release, but tradition says her spirit haunted the old grey tower of her wave-washed prison, and the music of her sweet voice used to float over the waters.

It comes upon us as a shock to find that the picturesque grim old fortress became in later years a salt works, and the ancient courtyard was used for a coal yard. Salt works and coal yards are practical parts of our everyday existence, but we could wish that the stately ruins of the past might be spared from such desecration, and that Narrowwater Castle had remained untouched.

A little in the northwest, there is a large stone in the middle of the river where two provinces meet, and an adventurous youth may stand upon three counties at once, Down, Armagh, and Louth, if he considers such a precarious venture repays the risk.

CHAPTER XXXVII

CROWN MOUNT

Crown Mount is a celebrated rath which lies one mile north-east of Newry. It stands 112 feet high, a large platform on the summit of a hill, and it is 600 feet in circumference.

The story of Crown Mount is an interesting one. It was erected as a place for single combat between two princes who each claimed a royal territory.

I shall try and tell the romantic old tale.

King Aengus—corrupted into MacGinness—had a son who was far beyond the bounds of Ulster. Prince Diarmid was famous for his beauty and ability, but still more for his noble deeds. He was a great sportsman and often passed far beyond his father's territory to hunt the savage wolf, wild boar and red deer, in the forests of Feudh Mor, "the Fews" and by the shores of Camlough, the "Crooked River". One day, when he was returning alone from the chase, he rode down the western hill into a village called Newry. On the banks of the Clanrye river, where there was a green dell surrounded by forest trees—on the identical spot where the barracks stand now—he saw a fair maiden milking her goats. He watched the most beautiful girl in Ireland, then, leaping from his horse, he begged for a drink.

Though she was clad in humble garments, she had an air of elegance and high descent. Everyone loved Mary O'Hanlon, and so did he, and as he led her to her cottage home, he begged her to accept his suit and become his queen in Iveagh. She refused, saying she was quite unfit for such a position. When the old woman she lived with heard who he was, she told him the secret of Mary's life. She was the child of the Prince of Ulster, and when her parents died, she was entrusted to the care of her mother's brother and his wife.

The nurse overheard a wicked plot for her death that the inheritance might fall to their own son. The nurse carried off the child and her jewels, and had kept her in that humble retreat. When she produced the jewels, Diarmid recognised them at once, and discovered that the lovely Mary was his own cousin. He challenged the usurper to single combat, which was fought at the Crown Mount Rath. Prince Diarmid of course won, and he lived long and happily ever after, and so ends the history of Crown Mount.

CHAPTER XXXVIII

CASTLE ROCHE

Castle Roche stands seven miles from Dundalk. It is built upon a great rock, and commands a most extensive view. The elevated position is rendered even more secure by the depth of the surrounding moat, while the immense strength of the walls renders it impregnable. With the single exception of Dunluce Castle, there is not a more imposing or massive ancient castle still in existence in the north of Ireland. There is a round tower which was in former times an outpost of the castle, and a secret passage once connected them. St. Ronan's Well lies near, and like so many ancient wells in Ireland, it is said to have possessed marvellous powers of healing, and thousands of pilgrims flocked to it constantly. As years advanced, these sacred waters lost—in some strange way—their miraculous gift of healing and in these later times their glory has departed. Nearer Dundalk, there is another place of intense interest—the hill of Foighard or Faughart which is where the last scene of Edward Bruce's ill-starred and romantic life took place.

We can sit here upon the very spot where he planted his standard almost seven hundred years ago. On this place on the 28th of May, 1318, the Scottish Chieftain and his followers stood, and raised his standard here. It nerved the heart of his tired soldiers, and raised their drooping spirits to look over the rich and beautiful country waiting—as they thought—to be theirs.

We are reminded of the story which is told of Oliver Cromwell when he stood on the rock of Cashel. He smiled grimly as his eyes traversed the golden vale of Tipperary, and his mind filled with thoughts of conquest and confiscation. Turning to his soldiers he said, "This is a land worth fighting for." We, too, may say in these later years, "This is a land worth living in." Turn which way we will, new beauties meet the eyes. The grim and timeworn mountains like great black lions guard the frontier, while at our feet the vivid green landscape lies laughing in the golden sunshine. It was here the hot and furious battle raged, and the English troops were crowned with victory. Edward Bruce died like a king. He engaged in combat with a Norman knight named Maupas, and, at the close of day, when the desperate conflict was over, they were found lying dead across each other.

The warriors who fell were all buried together, friend and foe alike. In an old churchyard at Faughart, in one great grave, they were laid "in one red burial blent." A huge granite slab covers the "King's Grave"—what king we know not.

The two brothers—both brave and fearless men, but blinded by ambition—were unfortunate. In the year 1819, in Dunfermline Abbey, was found under the slabs of royal tombs the skeleton of Robert Bruce.

It was wrapped in two coverings of thin sheet lead, rolled in a shroud of cloth of gold, all enclosed in an oak coffin which mouldered into dust. It was replaced in a lead coffin, and buried under the tower. In raised letters on the lid are these words

"King Robert Bruce, 1329-1819."

St. Bridget was born—some say—at Faughart, but at any rate she presided over a nunnery here on the ruins of which the old church was built. There is a well in the graveyard at the foot of an ancient ash tree, and it is marked by the possession of a most peculiar cup, which is a polished human skull. A drink from the holy well taken out of this remarkable cup was believed to cure toothache. One would like to know to whom the skull originally belonged. I would prefer a toothache, rather than such a revolting cure.

Castletown Castle was once a formidable stronghold and it still stands upon its island promontory. It was here that the brave and unfortunate Edward Bruce was crowned, and where he resided for two years.

An ancient story tells us that, when he came to be crowned, it was found there was no crown ready, and, as that was a most important part of the ceremonial, his followers were in a dilemma. One of them, more courageous than the others, disappeared for a short time, and returned bringing with him a golden crown.

He had ridden in hot haste to Dundalk, which was about one mile distant, and had begged the loan of the crown which was on the head of the figure of the Virgin Mary in the chapel there. After the coronation, it was sent back and placed upon the sacred figure again. It must have been rather small for Edward Bruce, but that was merely a detail, and it served the purpose for which it was required.

A little bit of old history is preserved quite near us, and brings to mind the stirring times of Queen Elizabeth. In a little

Presbyterian church, at Dundonald, the records and communion plate are kept in an old iron treasure chest. It came out of the Spanish ship which was wrecked at Dunluce. Another similar chest is preserved in the Tower of London, while two others are in Glenarm Castle. There is also, at Dundonald, a cromlech called the "Kempe Stones", which in Irish means "Eternal Homes", and a giant's grave. The ancient name of the place was "Baille-Clough-togal", the town of the strangers, now changed to "Greengraves".

It would require a more eloquent pen than mine, and larger space than can be given in this small book, to attempt to tell the story of all the ancient and interesting places near Belfast. The places which played a vigorous part and filled a large place in Irish history,—the beautiful old castles and fortresses which lie under the shadow of the Mourne Mountains along the shores of Carlingford Lough, and the lovely stretch of country surrounding Strangford,—and the old stories of Lough Neagh are full of a charm distinctly their own. Indeed, Dundrum alone would fill more pages than we can spare. On the other side, Dungannon, the ancient stronghold of the O'Neills, is overflowing with thrilling romance. Then the lovely glens of Antrim and the wilder scenery of the northern coast form a fit setting for many an old story.

An artist might spend a lifetime about Cushendall and the country on to Portrush and find fresh pictures every half-mile, and still leave undiscovered beauties for future generations to find out. No colours have ever been made, and no artist has ever been born who can give us the living light and shade on Lurigethan, or the exquisite indescribable beauty of the waves breaking on the rocks at Port-na-Spania. If such picture should ever be painted, this old world of ours will hold its breath, and be uplifted by such scenes.

We vibrate with the idea that it may have been in places like these—

> That the thought of Creation was born,
> Where the twilight of history touches the air,
> And the rivers the secret of Paradise share,
> Into the dawn of the world.

When these hills and rocks were formed fresh from the hands of the Creator, we can well imagine He looked down and said, "It is good," and on the seventh day He rested from all His labour.

FROM AN OLD POEM WRITTEN IN THE YEAR 1822

An Amphitheatre more grand,
Graces no part of Europe's land—
Where Neptune's elbow intervenes
To help the variegated scenes.

And over all the Hill of Caves,
With what a bold majestic pride
As if it heaven and earth defied,
The Fort looks o'er the space between,
To hills of yellow, red and green,

Even to old Scotia's craggy hills,
Chequered with sheep, cascades and rills,
To Carrick strongly fortified,
Defying French, and wind and tide,

And to Slieve Donard's airy height,
Which bounds the wearying southern height,
—Like Nature's beautified demesne.—
Those waving hills—that chequered plain,—
Thanks to thy stars, thou Queen of Towns,
Confirmed success thy labour crowns.

BIBLIOGRAPHY

The contents of this book have been gleaned from a large number of books, too numerous to mention, but the following are some of them.

Antiquities of Donegal	*O'Donovan*	
Antiquities of Ireland	*Sir James Ware*	1705
Belfast	*Benn*	
Book of Howth		
Carrickfergus	*Miskimmin*	
Christian Inscriptions	*Petrie*	
County Down	*Harrison*	
Derriana	*Bishop of Derry*	
Dictionary	*O'Brien*	
Farmer's Guide	*Dr. F. Moore*	1827
Giraldus Cambriensis		
History of County Down	*Knox*	
History of First Congregation 1805		
History of Ireland	*Warner*	
History of the O'Neills	*Matthews*	
Ireland	*Mrs. S. C. Hall*	
Ireland	*Sir Richard Musgrave*	1802
Ireland	*Earl Clarendon*	1621
Journey in Ireland	*Ingh*	1834

Bibliography

Lily of Medicine	*O'Hickey*	
Manners and Customs	*O'Curry*	
Manners and Customs of Hy-Fiachreach	*O'Hyne*	
Old Belfast Almanacks 1770-1829		
Pacata Hibernia		
Parish of Holywood	*O'Laverty*	
Picturesque Ireland	*Thomas Cromwell*	1820
Political History of Ireland	*Mullata*	1793
Round Towers	*Petrie*	
Statistical Surveys		
Strangers in Ireland		1805
The Antient and Present State of the County of Down	*Harris*	1744
The Cromwellian Settlement in Ireland	*John P. Prendergast*	
The Four Masters		
Three Town Books of Belfast	*Young*	
Topographical History	*Lewis*	
Tour in Ireland, 1776	*Young*	
Ulster Journal of Archaeology		

The charm and enjoyment which the reader will derive from this printing of *The Story of Belfast and Its Surroundings* are a result of the author's celebration of history, her thoughts on the future and on posterity, and the 'modern world's' reaction to such clear-headed thought. Writing as a modern twentieth-century woman, the author at times puts herself in the person of someone a century past, and wonders at the technology and industry at her fingertips. As readers we feel the thrill of seeing the future, the past and a further past simultaneously: the 1913 publication gives twenty-first century readers a sense of the passing nature of modern technology, whatever the date.

The passage of time makes liars of us all: facts in one age may be disproved or clarified. There are a few innacuracies or mistaken attributions in the 1913 edition, which we feel bound to address. Language has developed or diverged, to the point where meanings which would have been perfectly clear at the beginning of the twentieth century bear close explanation at the beginning of the twenty-first. None of the corrections or revisions should detract from the text as originally printed.

A<small>DDENDA</small> / E<small>RRATA</small> <small>TO THE</small> 1913 <small>EDITION</small>

A<small>CKNOWLEDGEMENTS</small>
[1] ***Messrs. Macaw, etc.*** McCaw, Stevenson & Orr (it is unknown whether the 'parrot' reference was deliberate!)

I<small>NTRODUCTION</small>
[1] ***Madhigan*** The usual spelling is now 'Madigan'

C<small>HAPTER</small> I
[1] ***"Joy" Street*** Named for the Joy family, who were involved in printing works, publishing and linen in the early years of these industries in Belfast
[2] ***"Happy are the people who have no history"*** George Eliot wrote in *The Mill on the Floss* that "the happiest women, like the happiest nations, have no history."
[3] ***Bel-Feirste*** 'Béal Feirste' is the more usual spelling
[4] ***fortalices*** structures for defence; small forts
[5] ***Sir Moses Hill*** Sir Moyses Hill (died 1629)
[6] ***three hundred and fifty years*** The author was writing in 1912, commenting on 1663 a date over 250 years distant; unless she meant to address the readership of her book in the 21st century!
[7] ***perquisite*** a claimed right or benefit (sometimes vulgarly abbreviated to 'perk' – as in 'a perk of the job')
[8] ***street arabs*** vagrant or street children

Chapter II
[1] ***alterage*** Correctly 'altarage'; a stipend or 'tithe', not as stated

in the book 'a small church'. The significance of the church is not affected by this change, as the greater number of tithes owed, reflected the importance or significance of the church organisation.

[2] *St. Anne's Cathedral* The foundation stone was laid in 1889, and in 2004 the nave celebrated the centenary of its consecration.

Chapter III

[1] *the Spanish war* The War of the Spanish Succession (1701-1714)

Chapter IV

[1] *calendering* A process in which a fabric is heated, rolled and pressed to give a shiny surface.

Chapter VI

[1] *atmospheric system* stretches of railway track using pneumatic means to propel trains and carriages, rather than by steam power alone.

[2] *gyroscopic railway* a system proposed by Irishman Louis Brennan in the early twentieth century. He also patented a steerable torpedo, in 1877.

[3] *Dunlop* John Boyd Dunlop, a Scottish veterinarian and inventor who lived in Belfast for a time.

[4] *McAdam* The author mistakenly attributes the invention of tarmacadam to Robert Shipboy MacAdam, a Belfast businessman who is now best known as an antiquarian, and

collector of Gaelic manuscripts. The Scottish inventor and road surface innovator John MacAdam was born in 1756, while the Irish antiquarian was born in 1808. They were unrelated. (The Victorian/Edwardian penchant for claiming human progress as uniquely local–British/Irish or from Belfast, it does not much matter–may be at work here).

Chapter VII
[1] *uncalled-for* Uncollected, not 'unwarranted' or 'undeserved'.

Chapter IX
[1] *consumption* an early name for the lung disease 'tuberculosis'

Chapter XI
[1] *money at the present time* Following decimalisation in 1971, the old £sd system (pounds, shillings, pence) was altered so that 100 pence=£1, a shilling=5p, a penny=1p. Until decimalisation in 1971, British currency values were was as follows:
1/2d. Half penny. £1 = 480 halfpennies
1d. one pence (penny). £1 = 240 pennies
3d. three pence (thruppence). £1 = 80 thrupenny bits
sixpence There were 2 sixpence to a shilling. £1 = 40 sixpences
shilling There were 12 pence in a shilling. £1 = 20 shillings
half-a-crown two shillings and sixpence. £1 = 8 half-crowns

Chapter XII
[1] *inch of candle* A unit, measurement of time: the time it takes for an inch-high length of candle to burn down.

[2] **ankers** An anker is a liquid measure: equivalent to 8 ½ imperial gallons (38.6 litres).

[3] **goloshes** previous spelling of 'galoshes', or overshoes.

Chapter XIV

[1] **Ballydrain House** The Montgomery family connection persisted until 1918. In 1960 the estate was purchased by Malone Golf Club.

[2] **[Purdysburn] Lunatic Asylum** Now renamed 'Knockbracken Healthcare Park.

[3] **souterrain** An underground passageway or enclosure ('sous' in French is 'under' or 'beneath').

[4] **Belvoir Park** since 1961, Belvoir Forest Park.

Chapter XV

[1] **a different name** perhaps 'pirate' rather than 'privateer' (which denotes an individual or ship engaged by a government to disrupt shipping - almost piracy with a state's agreement).

[2] **Spiked the guns** Driving a spike into the firing 'mechanism' of a cannon, preventing it from discharging – rendering it useless.

[3] **Carrickfergus Roads** an area of Belfast Lough just off the coastal town.

[4] **almost completed** the fort was operational from 1907-1960.

[5] **at this time** from 1778 onwards.

Chapter XVI

[1] **Well-known Belfast writer** Alice Milligan (1866-1953).

[2] **Vallum** a defensive earthwork wall.

Chapter XVII

[1] **Ballyclare...paper-mills** the mills at Ballyclare lasted until after the Second World War.

[2] **Queen Elizabeth** Elizabeth I (1533-1603).

[3] **shagreen** originally horse-leather, now more commonly derived from ray or shark skin.

[4] **vitriol works** manufacture of sulphuric acid for industrial processes.

Chapter XVIII

[1] **mentioned in "Hero and Leander"** Actually in Byron's "Don Juan"; the swim took place October 10th 1810.

Chapter XX

[1] **cwt** One hundredweight (51 kg)

[2] **statue of Harland** In addition to the statue of Sir William Harland, there is now a memorial to those who perished in the wreck of the *Titanic*.

Chapter XXII

[1] **Henry Kirke White** The poem is "Time, a poem". The poet lived from 1785-1806.

[2] **rus in urbe** countryside in the town (Latin).

Chapter XXIII

[1] The extract is from a poem "The Geraldines" written by Thomas Davis (1814-1845).

Chapter XXIV
[1] *The Goban Saor* Legendary-to-mythical builder of castles and fortifications in Ireland.
[2] *Dean Swift's rectory* the building was demolished in 1959 following a fire. The area is now the Kilroot power station.

Chapter XXV
[1] *Vallancey* General Charles Vallancey, writer, antiquarian and co-founder of the Royal Irish Academy.
[2] *scold/skold* one who criticises, heckles, annoys: a public nuisance, generally but not exclusively a woman.

Chapter XXVII
[1] *Colombkille* also 'Columbkille', 'Columcille' etc.

Chapter XXVIII
[1] *Jeannie Watt's cave* now called 'Jenny Watts' cave'.

Chapter XXX
[1] *Coud Castle* also known as 'Cowd' or 'Choud' castle.
[2] *railway may...* the railway line to Ardglass closed in the 1950s.

Chapter XXXI
[1] *Dun-Padriug* Dun-Padraig (more commonly).

Chapter XXXII
[1] *Morice McLoghlin* Maurice McLoughlin, King of Ireland.

Chapter XXXIII
¹ Ulster Apennines the author refers to the Mourne Mountains.

Chapter XXXV
¹ candles...1300 the date is disputed: the author claims 1300,
but other sources list candles or candlestick types from B.C.
Paris tax lists detail the existence of chandlers in 1290s.
² Gerona the galleass *Girona*, lost 1588.
³ Port-na-Spania 'Spanish Bay', named for wreck of ship of the
Spanish Armada, 16th century.
⁴ Chalybeate containing iron
⁵ last Irish giant Patrick Murphy (1834-1862): at his tallest
reported height, he reached 8ft 1in.

BIBLIOGRAPHY
Belfast
'A History of the Town of Belfast' by George Benn (1877)
Carrickfergus
'The History and Antiquities of the County of the Town of
Carrickfergus' by Samuel Miskimmin
Giraldus Cambriensis
Giraldus Cambrensis (12th-century writings on Ireland)
History of County Down
'A History of the County Down' by Dr. Alexander Knox (1875)
Ireland: Its Scenery, Character &c. Mr. & Mrs S. C. Hall
(1841)
'Memoirs of the Different Rebellions in Ireland' by Sir Richard
Musgrave (1802)

Prendergast
John P. Prendergast (1870)
Strangers in Ireland
may in fact be 'The Stranger in Ireland...' by Sir John Carr
Journey in Ireland
may in fact be 'A Journey Throughout Ireland during the
Spring, Summer, and Autumn of 1834' by Henry D. Inglis
History of Ireland by Ferdinando Warner, 1763
Pacata Hibernia or 'A History of the Wars in Ireland' ed.
Standish O'Grady (1896?)
Matthews Anthony Mathews
Hy-Fiachreach may be 'Hy-Fiachrach', and author/translator
may be 'John O'Donovan'
Topographical History 'Topographical Dictionary of Ireland'
by Samuel Lewis (1837)
'Excursions through Ireland: comprising topographical
and historical delineations of each province; together with
descriptions of the residences of the nobility and gentry,
remains of antiquity, and every other object of interest or
curiosity; forming a complete guide for the traveller
and tourist; illustrated with engravings' by Thomas Cromwell
(1820)
Round Towers
'Round Towers of Ireland' by George Petrie
Christian Inscriptions
'Christian Inscriptions in the Irish Language' by George Petrie
Bishop of Derry
John Graham, author of 'Derriana' (1823)